To Eric:

[signature]

Isa.
61:1

"Got struggles? Then *Mountain in My Rearview Mirror* is the book for you. Bill Butterworth weaves humor and powerful stories together with solid help for those who feel overwhelmed. It's enjoyable, helpful, and nobody tells a story like Bill. I heartily recommend it!"

LEE STROBEL
Author of The Case for the Real Jesus

"Life struggles are unavoidable, and they can range from minor frustrations to major losses. But God has a path and a plan that can bring you into a better life than you had before. In *Mountain in My Rearview Mirror*, Bill Butterworth provides substance, hope, and practical answers for those dealing with the obstacles that affect us all. His book will inspire and guide you."

JOHN TOWNSEND
Psychologist, speaker, and author of
Boundaries *and* Who's Pushing Your Buttons?

"Bill Butterworth has had some mountains to climb in his life. We all have—or will soon. And when we're facing the uphill challenges of life, we want an experienced guide beside us—one who can provide the coaching and encouragement to get us over the tough parts and get back to enjoying fullness of life. You'll find the reality and wisdom in Bill's book to be the very thing to help you face the highest hurdles before you."

JOHN TRENT, PhD
President, The Center for StrongFamilies
Author of The Blessing *and* The 2 Degree Difference

"When facing mountains, you want guidance and encouragement from one who has been in the valley but also scaled the heights. Bill Butterworth is that person, and *Mountain in My Rearview Mirror* is the book. With humor, real-life illustrations, and biblical wisdom, Bill shows us how to overcome—and put behind us—the seemingly insurmountable obstacles in our own lives."

MARK MITTELBERG
Author of Becoming a Contagious Church *and* Choosing Your Faith

"There is no question about it: We all face difficult times. But Bill Butterworth offers us a map to guide us through those times when we think the obstacles are too great to overcome. Bill is a fellow traveler, a guide, who will show you that not only can you make it through your tough times but that you will come out the other side stronger and better."

BILL DALLAS

CEO, The Church Communication Network

"As a speaker, Bill has famously brought thousands of live audiences to laughter and tears. And I'm glad to say Bill's writing is exactly like Bill's speaking: very funny, very smart, and very, very relevant. The GTO story alone is worth the price of this book! Bill has a way of sneaking up on you—one minute you're in hysterics over his description of a childhood faux pas, and the next minute you're realizing a life-transforming spiritual insight."

RENE SCHLAEPFER

Conference speaker and senior pastor
Twin Lakes Church, Aptos, California

"*Mountain in My Rearview Mirror* is brimming with hope, encouragement, compassion, and realism. Bill shows the way to overcoming adversity as only one who has been through it can. In doing so, he's as likely to have you laughing as crying. Don't miss this book!"

JUD WILHITE

Author of Stripped: Uncensored Grace on the Streets of Vegas
Senior pastor, Central Christian Church, Las Vegas

"In his latest book, *Mountain in My Rearview Mirror*, Bill Butterworth once again opens up his life to us in his winsome and powerful way. I appreciate Bill's incredible ability to communicate with authenticity and wisdom. As you read this book—on an airplane, in a coffee shop, or on your break at work—you will want to warn people around you that laughter or even a shout of 'You're absolutely right, Bill' may burst forth at any time."

ERIC HEARD

Pastor, Mariners Church, Irvine, California

"Once again, Bill Butterworth delivers practical hope in equal measures of help, perspective, and inspiration. *Mountain in My Rearview Mirror* is an incredible resource for us mere mortals journeying on this trouble-filled road trip called life."

MIKE HOWERTON
Lead pastor, Overlake Christian Church, Redmond, Washington

"The introduction to this book says, 'This book is punctuated with the power of story.' Yes, and it is accented by the delights of humor. Bill Butterworth is one of the funniest guys I have ever known—and one of the best storytellers. He uses these rare gifts to communicate life-changing truth from God's Word. As you read this book, you will laugh, and you will cry—and you will grow."

BOB THUNE
Senior pastor, Southwest Community Church, Indian Wells, California

MOUNTAIN
IN MY REARVIEW
MIRROR

A Guide to

Overcoming

Overwhelming

Obstacles

BILL BUTTERWORTH

 TYNDALE HOUSE PUBLISHERS, INC., CAROL STREAM, ILLINOIS

Visit Tyndale's exciting Web site at www.tyndale.com

TYNDALE and Tyndale's quill logo are registered trademarks of Tyndale House Publishers, Inc.

Mountain in My Rearview Mirror: A Guide to Overcoming Overwhelming Obstacles

Copyright © 2008 by Bill Butterworth. All rights reserved.

Cover photograph of mountains copyright © by Photodisc. All rights reserved.

Cover photograph of hand and mirror by Stephen Vosloo copyright © by Tyndale House Publishers, Inc. All rights reserved.

Interior illustrations of hands copyright © by iStockphoto. All rights reserved.

Interior illustrations of mountains copyright © by Brandon Laufenberg/iStockphoto. All rights reserved.

Designed by Stephen Vosloo

Published in association with the literary agency of Alive Communications, Inc., 7680 Goddard Street, Suite 200, Colorado Springs, CO 80920. www.alivecommunications.com

Unless otherwise indicated, all Scripture quotations are taken from the *New American Standard Bible*®, copyright © 1960, 1962, 1963, 1968, 1971, 1972, 1973, 1975, 1977, 1995 by The Lockman Foundation. Used by permission.

Scripture quotations marked NLT are taken from the *Holy Bible,* New Living Translation, copyright © 1996, 2004. Used by permission of Tyndale House Publishers, Inc., Carol Stream, Illinois 60188. All rights reserved.

Library of Congress Cataloging-in-Publication Data

Butterworth, Bill.
  Mountain in my rearview mirror : a guide to overcoming overwhelming obstacles / Bill Butterworth.
    p. cm.
  ISBN-13: 978-1-4143-1567-6 (hc)
  ISBN-10: 1-4143-1567-8 (hc)
1. Suffering—Religious aspects—Christianity.   I. Title.
  BV4909.B89 2008
  248.8′6—dc22   2007030255

Printed in the United States of America

13   12   11   10   09   08
 7   6   5   4   3   2   1

For Gary and Linda Bender

*Thanks for all you taught me on that
climb up Camelback Mountain*

TABLE OF
CONTENTS

ACKNOWLEDGMENTS

A BOOK IS always a collaborative effort; therefore, I have many people to thank who have invested in my life. In countless ways they have made a great contribution to this book.

Don Pape stoked my creative juices for this project. I always appreciate how he listens to all my wild ideas.

The folks at Tyndale House are fantastic. It has been such an enriching experience to get to know some of them like: Doug Knox, Jan Long Harris, Nancy Clausen, Sarah Atkinson, Bonne Steffen, Stephen Vosloo, and Sharon Leavitt.

I have wonderful friends in my life. I am so grateful to people like Lee and Leslie Strobel, Joe and Molly

Davis, Mike and Marcia Scott, Ron and Kay Nelson, Bob and Barb Ludwig, Gary and Linda Bender, Jim and Ines Franklin, Al and Anita Manley, Todd and Cheryl Jensen, Bob and Lori Harron, and Trish Guzman for their valuable contributions on a regular basis.

I have a men's study group that I meet with regularly who have been a help and encouragement beyond what I could write on this page. Thanks so much, guys!

Many pastors have helped me along the way with their friendship and counsel. I am grateful for Bill Hybels, Rick Warren, Kenton Beshore, Jud Wilhite, Ray Johnston, Rene Schlaepfer, Eric Heard, and Mike Howerton.

Our family continues to grow, and they are truly my greatest treasure. Thank you to Justin and Joy Leslie and their children, Jill and Jenna; Jesse and Marisa Butterworth and their children, Liam and Finn; Jeffrey and Sarah Butterworth and their daughter, Ava: John Butterworth, Lisa White; and Joseph Butterworth. You are all pure inspiration to me.

And finally, my dear wife, Kathi. In many ways, you are the embodiment of what it means to overcome overwhelming obstacles. I am so blessed to have you in my life.

INTRODUCTION

THE LESSON FROM CLIMBING CAMELBACK MOUNTAIN

YEARS AGO SOMEONE told me in a public speaking class, "If you speak to the hurting, you will never lack for an audience."

I have never forgotten that adage, yet I have to admit I didn't jump on it as soon as I heard it. Why? Because when I first heard those words I wasn't hurting. Not only was I not hurting, to the best of my recollection, I had never been hurting in any sort of significant manner up to that time in my life.

However, God, in His providence, allowed my life to come crashing down several years later.

As soon as I began to hurt, I realized the power in that quote. People in pain find great comfort from those who also have experienced pain. Upon reflection, I realized how "charmed" a life I had led up to that point. Happy marriage, healthy children, rising career, no major illnesses—life was good.

Then my marriage ended. I knew we had had our struggles in our seventeen years together, but I didn't see the divorce coming. We tried to end it as amicably as possible, attempting as best we could to pay attention to our kids and how they would be affected. Needless to say, since I was making my living primarily as a speaker on marriage and family issues, the end of our marriage sent my career into a tailspin. I crashed and burned. I was convinced I would never again be happy, healthy, and whole. It was an obstacle I felt I could not overcome.

However, this is not a book about divorce recovery. It's bigger than that. It's a book about the basics of rising from the ashes. It's a look at putting the pieces back together. It's a series of lessons on overcoming overwhelming obstacles.

In the midst of my recovery from the early stages of my personal trauma, an event occurred that continues to teach me things about myself to this day. It's a marvelous metaphor for me—and I hope for you.

My world had dramatically changed, and I was crushed against an overwhelming obstacle. I wanted to be alone so I could cry, so I could grieve, so I could feel sorry for myself. I didn't want to deal with anything or anyone; I spent hours curled up on the couch in the fetal position.

The telephone became a real intruder. Because I was totally depleted of all energy, both physical and emotional, I didn't want to pick up the phone and explain to yet one more person how my life was dredging below rock bottom.

Thank goodness for my answering machine. When I would hear the voice of someone with whom I wanted to connect recording a message, I would pick up the receiver.

One autumn morning my good friend Gary Bender called. Our friendship goes back a long way, yet often our lives got so busy that blocks of time would slip by without either of us realizing it. As I heard Gary's voice on my answering machine, I realized we had not spoken since I had become single again. Taking a deep breath, I picked up the phone. "Hi, Gary, I'm here. I'm just screening my calls," I sheepishly admitted.

"How's it going, friend?" he asked. "It's been a long time since we've talked. Bring me up to date."

"Well, I hope you're sitting down," I began. "Updating you on how I'm doing may include some surprising news."

And with that I launched into the whole story of my personal catastrophe. Gary was stunned.

"Bill, I had no idea" was about all he could say initially.

"I know, Gary. No one had any idea. I've been doing a pretty good job of keeping to myself these days. I'm just so embarrassed by this whole series of events. I don't know any other way to handle it."

As he started to regain his composure, Gary asked me, "So what can Linda and I do for you?"

"Pray" was the only thing I could think of at that moment. "And keep being my friend."

"Are you busy over the next few weeks?" he asked sincerely. When I explained that I was facing the accompanying obstacle of being virtually unemployed, he understood I had plenty of time on my hands.

"So you're just kind of hanging out?"

"Yeah," I replied, realizing how sad it sounded. "I'm just hanging out."

We talked for a few more minutes. When I hung up the phone, I remember thinking, *Well, that didn't go very well!* Here I was, pouring my heart out to my friend, and all he really seemed to care about was that I was hanging out all by myself.

The next day it all made sense.

Around 10:30, a FedEx guy was knocking on my front door. He delivered an envelope from Gary containing a round-trip plane ticket to Phoenix, where Gary and his wife, Linda, lived.

I speed-dialed Gary's number. "What's this all about?"

"Linda and I want you to come out and spend a few days with us," he explained. "We think you could use a little change of pace. Linda will be here when you arrive, but the next day she will be leaving to visit a friend in Colorado, so you and I will have a few days to be a couple of bachelors. I figure we should do bachelor things like play a lot of golf, eat barbecued ribs, and raise our cholesterol!"

Before I could respond, he added, "Please don't turn me down, Bill. You know you'd do the same thing for me if the tables were turned." And then he added the big line: "No one should have to go through what you're going through *alone*."

So that's how I ended up in Phoenix. Gary and I played lots of golf, ate a ton of ribs, and sent our cholesterol levels off the chart. It really was just what I needed. The change of scenery did me good, and even better was the fact that there was someone in my life who wanted to help me.

The night before I was supposed to leave, Gary poked his head into the guest room where I had already retired for the night. "We really had a good time, didn't we?" he said with unbridled enthusiasm.

"Yeah, Gary, this whole trip has been great!" I replied honestly.

"Well, I have one more idea before you get out of here," he continued.

"What's up?" I asked.

"Okay, your flight home isn't until tomorrow afternoon, right?"

"That's right," I replied. "It's not till around four."

"Perfect. Whaddya say tomorrow morning we get up real early and drive out to the base of Camelback Mountain? We can climb the mountain and see the sun rise over Phoenix. It is breathtaking—it'll change your life!"

I hesitated for a second. Would this really change my life? Besides, Gary was a jock and I had the athletic prowess of tile grout. What he thought might be easy could be flirting with death for me. But how could I refuse without looking like a complete weenie?

"Okay, Gary, it sounds good to me!" I gushed, hoping my fake enthusiasm wasn't detectable.

Immediately, I knew I was in trouble when Gary started throwing together gear for the hike. Hiking boots, loose-fitting shorts and shirts, and my favorite piece of equipment—a belt with eight plastic water bottles attached to it with Velcro.

"Tomorrow I am going to die," I concluded, and with

that I decided I should at least get a good night's sleep before it happened.

The next morning proved to be one of the most amazing adventures of my life.

We awoke at o-dark-thirty and drove to the base of the mountain. If nothing else, dressed in my hiking gear, I at least looked the part.

"Are you sure you're up to this?" Gary asked as we stretched our leg muscles in preparation for the hike.

"No problem," I lied. "I'm in great shape—I take the trash cans down to the end of the driveway once a week."

While we were warming up, it quickly became obvious that Gary and I weren't the only two people with the cool idea of climbing Camelback to see the sunrise. Literally dozens of people were streaming toward the mountain, forming a human chain winding its way up the slope.

I also noticed that this line of humanity was *old*. Yes, the senior partners of the AARP were on patrol, presiding over this predawn ritual much like they had done when Calvin Coolidge was president.

When we finished warming up, Gary got in line behind a dear old gent, and I followed behind my friend. I started off strong, actually feeling exhilarated by the entire experience.

Then I got to the third minute of the hike.

That's right. It only took me a little over two minutes

to feel the cornucopia of pain that was beginning in my body. My thighs were screaming. My lungs felt like they were going to explode. I was light-headed. Worst of all, every drop of water in all eight water bottles was drained dry.

Obviously my pace had slowed down to a crawl. The senior behind me didn't like that development one bit. "Get the (blankety-blank) out of the line if you can't keep up, you (blankety-blank)!" I was surprised to hear such ripe profanity from a ninety-year-old, leather-skinned, bow-legged, tattooed, chain-smoking, blue-haired woman.

At her recommendation, I gladly stepped out of line. I was coughing, wheezing, and watching the mountain swirl around me in my predeath gaze.

"Are you okay, Bill?" Gary asked, genuinely concerned.

By now the whole scene seemed like something out of a movie script. So in my best Hollywood voice, I said, "Go ahead, Gary—save yourself. On the way back down, if the buzzards haven't eaten my body, take it back with you. And tell my kids I love 'em, okay?"

"Come on now, Bill, relax," Gary encouraged. "You just need a little rest. You can do it!"

"No, I can't," I replied.

"Yes, you can."

"*No* . . . I can't."

"Yes, you can."

"*No . . .* I *can't!*" I finally blurted out in utter exasperation.

By now Gary could see that I was serious, so he paused for a moment and then changed tactics.

"What if we climbed this mountain *at your pace?*" he suggested. "We could go as slow or as fast as you wanted. We could stop and rest whenever you needed. I really think you need to get to the top of this mountain, buddy. So what do you say?"

All I could think of in response was "Well, if we do that . . . we won't see the sun rise!"

Gary smiled, patted me on the shoulder, and said, "Come on, let's keep going on our journey."

And with that we started our slow, steady, lengthy hike up Camelback Mountain. Throughout the hike, Gary would stop and share his water with me, since I had foolishly drunk all mine in the first two minutes. What a friend! *No one should have to go through this alone* kept running through my mind.

Ultimately we made it to the top. Gary and I were exuberant over our accomplishment. And we were both correct in statements we had made earlier in the morning. I had accurately predicted that we would not see the sun rise. By the time we got to the peak, we had a "Phoenix at high noon" thing going on.

But Gary was right too. The hike changed my life. Sure, the view of the city of Phoenix was breathtaking.

But more important, I did it! At a time in my life when I felt as if I couldn't do anything right, I had achieved a pretty cool goal.

I looked at Gary, who was beaming broadly. He was so proud of me. I wanted to do something to make this an occasion I would never forget.

"Gary, would you do me a favor?" I asked as an idea dawned on me. "Would you take a minute while we're on this mountaintop and just say a little prayer for me and my kids? It would really mean a lot to me."

He nodded, and right there, in the midst of God's glorious splendor, my friend prayed that I would be able to overcome this overwhelming obstacle.

It was a short prayer. It was nothing exceptionally eloquent or grandiose. But by the time he said "Amen," I was weeping.

After a few more moments of taking in the view, we started down the mountain. I soon learned that going *down* a mountain is not all that difficult. I could keep a healthy pace. I could take in all the sights. I could even carry on a bit of a conversation at the same time!

That trip up Camelback symbolized my life, and it also symbolizes yours. Life is a mountain journey. All of us are somewhere on that journey.

Some of us are on the way up the mountain—probably most of you who are reading these words right now. Your life is tough. You are tired, fatigued, near exhaustion.

Emotionally, your thighs are screaming and your lungs are about to explode. And you feel as if you have totally depleted all the water in your emotional tank. You think it just can't hurt any worse than it does now.

My hope in writing this book is that you'll see that you can get to the top of the mountain, where a new experience awaits you. What I gained at the top of Camelback Mountain can be summed up in one key word:

Perspective.

Had I seen the skyline of Phoenix before? Yes. Had I ever seen it from that perspective? No. And what did I have to do in order to gain that perspective? Endure the pain of climbing the mountain.

Honestly, I see things in my life today that I never would have seen without the opportunity to overcome the overwhelming obstacles in my life. I'm a different man—a better man—today. For all the theologians out there, let me be clear. I don't think God caused my obstacles, but He certainly did allow them to happen. And I think He did so in order to strengthen me in the way I live my life. He was building character.

There is another spot you might be on this mountain: working your way back down. Life is going pretty well right now. Life is good. The pace is such that you can even stop to smell the roses.

Of course, life is more than one mountain journey. It feels as if no sooner do we get past one obstacle than we are met head-on by another, and the mountain climb begins all over again.

That's the way it works. That's life.

My hope is that what you discover in the following pages will help you navigate difficult terrain: despair and discord, fear and doubt, guilt and shame, and overwhelming adversity.

This book is punctuated with the power of story. Just as the climb up Camelback Mountain has stayed with me, I believe stories stay with us light-years longer than bullet points do. Oh, I'll make some points; you don't have to worry about that. But my goal is to give you the water you desperately crave on your eventful life hike.

And, of course, I'd like to help you gain a new perspective as well.

ONE

CHAPTER

THE LESSON FROM THE CHURCH BASKETBALL LEAGUE

IN HIGH SCHOOL I yearned to be an athlete. The "cool" kids in school were all jocks, and most teenage boys aspired to be as cool as them. Unfortunately, my swim in the DNA pool left me with abs resembling a doughnut rather than a six-pack. I was tubby—that's the kindest way to put it.

So in school my lot was cast as a member of the marching band. Now, I'm sure marching band is cool in many schools, but in ours it was definitely on the opposite end of the popularity chain. Besides an interest in throwing the shot put and the discus for the track team, I found an outlet for my athletic aspirations . . . the church league.

It's true. I was a regular participant in church softball, church flag football, and of course, church basketball.

Two stars on the church basketball team, Teddy and Gary, were starters on our high school varsity basketball team. Not only were Teddy and Gary big men on campus, but they were also two of my closest friends. I idolized both of them. When Teddy asked me to join the church league, I felt I was one step closer to the cool life.

But there was still one problem. I possessed the athletic ability of a doorknob.

So the good news was that I was on the church basketball team. (Many years later I learned that the church team had a "no cut" policy, as a way to be an example of Christian love.) The bad news is that I sat on the bench every game—no exaggeration.

There just never seemed to be the right opportunity to put me in as a substitute for a good player. (In reality, even though we had a team made up of some exceptional players, there was never a game where the coach felt we had a large enough lead to put the entire game in jeopardy by sending me onto the court.)

But like any good tale of youthful innocence run amok, there was this one game. . . .

It was a snowy Tuesday evening in March, the Philadelphia weather at its worst. Our little band of church boys bravely boarded the church bus for the treacherous three-mile ride to our opponents' church gymnasium. It was a lone rectangular building at the back end of the parking lot. The building was literally the same size as a basketball court, with just enough room on the sidelines for eight to ten loyal fans to squeeze in and watch. The baskets that hung on opposite ends were just a few feet from the small, thin pads placed on the walls to soften the blow if a player ran too far down the court.

We hustled out of the bus and quickly scrambled into the heated gym. My teammates and I were wearing only sweatshirts and sweatpants over our uniforms, so it felt as if the frigid temperature had penetrated down to our bones' marrow. We needed no motivation to begin warm-ups. We were freezing; layup drills were the equivalent of steaming cups of hot cocoa.

I reveled in the pregame warm-ups because they were usually the only playing time I ever saw. Then the game began and I obediently took my usual place on the bench—all the way at the end, the player farthest from the coach.

The game progressed pretty much as usual. Having two starting high school varsity players on our church team made us relatively unbeatable. But soon it became apparent that this night was going to be different. Our opponents had a player who was actually quite good. As carefully as our team attempted to defend him, he always seemed to elude their grasp, break free, and score two points.

That's precisely when Teddy hatched his plan.

During a time-out, Teddy walked to my end of the bench. "Butterworth, are you ready to get a little playing time?" he asked in an almost seductive tone.

"You'd better believe I'm ready," I replied, not fully believing what my ears were hearing.

"Okay, good," Teddy continued in a hushed tone, almost a whisper. "At the next time-out, I'm going to ask the coach to put you in."

"You are?" I was in shock.

"Yes, but there is a specific reason why I want you in there. We need a big guy like you to defend their star player."

"You do?" I was mystified by Teddy's strategy, and he knew it. So he clarified. "Yeah, the next time he gets the ball and you are defending him, I want you to give him an intentional foul. Do you know what that means?"

"I think so. It means I foul him on purpose, right?"

"Exactly. We do it to send a message. And the message is 'Don't mess around with us!'"

"Okay," I stammered.

"So that means when you foul him, you've got to really foul him. You got it?"

"Yeah," I said. My assignment became crystal clear. I was being put in to use my extra tonnage as a weapon—a lethal weapon.

The referee blew the whistle, and the teams were back out on the floor. On the bench, I was sweating peanut butter, facing a moral dilemma of gargantuan proportions. I was finally being allowed to play in a game, but my assignment was a sinister one at best. I had never been a fan of the intentional foul, and now I was being asked to deliver one.

I began praying that the other team's star would suddenly grow stone-cold at the basket. The kid was on fire.

As the scores grew ominously closer on the scoreboard, I heard our coach shout, "Time!" I was completely drenched in sweat, even though I had barely moved a muscle sitting on the bench. I saw Teddy conferring with the coach. They looked down the bench, staring at me.

"Butterworth, come here," the coach barked. I hustled down as fast as a wide body could move. "Are you ready to play a little basketball?"

"Put me in, Coach!" I hoped he was going to ask me to play a little man-to-man defense on their worst player.

"See number twelve out there?" the coach continued. "I want you to guard him. And the next time he gets the ball, I want you to foul him. Got it? Foul him!"

I nodded, but my heart wasn't in it. The knots in my stomach made my heart inaccessible.

Teddy saw my uncertainty, and he came over to psych me up. "Bill, you can do this. You are going in to replace me so we can really foul this guy. If you get nervous, I want you to look over at me on the bench. I will help you get through it, okay?"

I nodded.

"Just remember, Bill," Teddy continued, "we're number one!" He held up the index finger of his right hand, the familiar "number one" gesture that we all knew, embedding in my brain the sign of victory.

I smiled weakly and slowly walked onto the court, feeling more like a convicted murderer being led to his execution than a church-league player. I looked over at Teddy; he was smiling, confident, making the number one sign. At that moment I didn't feel like number one. I didn't like where this plan was going. All I could think to do was to gesture back at Teddy. Since it was the late 1960s, I responded with my index finger and third finger spread, not in a V for victory, but in the universal sign of the sixties . . . *peace*!

Teddy wasn't pleased with my peace sign, so he changed gestures. He held his right thumb straight up at me. "Thumbs-up," his hand was saying. It was the ultimate sign of hope.

I am sure this nonverbal conversation only took a matter of seconds, but I've never forgotten it.

The ref blew his whistle to resume the game. It was

our ball. Gary threw it to my friend Bobby from under our basket. It was at that moment that number twelve from the opposing team seemed to leap out from nowhere and magically steal the ball from us. With our team in shock, he sped down the court all by himself. This was my moment. This was my destiny.

With all the speed I could muster (okay, me and speed might be an oxymoron), I took off after number twelve to accomplish my goal. Because he didn't see me, or else he didn't take me seriously, he slowed down to make an easy layup.

It was just enough of a delay to get me to the point of contact. I used all my body weight and drove it into his midsection, just as he was ascending to the basket.

I hit him. I hit him hard. His body hurtled under the basket and crashed into the thinly padded wall. He seemed to stay glued to the wall for just a second, and then he slid down like wet mud oozing down the side of a cliff.

He was out cold.

I turned away. I looked at my bench. Our coach was looking at me with shocked horror. Teddy was beaming from ear to ear.

The next thing I heard was a gut-wrenching moan from our opponents' coach. *"What have you done? What have you done?"* I knew he would be upset losing his star player, but what he said next completely threw me.

"What have you done to my son!"

Hurting a player was bad enough. But I had creamed the coach's son. This is not a good move under the best of circumstances, but being the visiting team, I knew the situation would only get worse.

"I want this kid ejected from the game!" the coach/father instructed the referee, as he pointed directly at me.

The ref nodded in agreement.

"Not only do I want him ejected, I want him out of my gym!"

The ref agreed again.

Before my coach could return to his senses, I was escorted out of the gym, which meant that I was escorted outside.

Outside . . .

in the snow . . .

wearing only a tank top, shorts, and sneakers.

And perhaps a thousand pounds of blubber.

It was a difficult way to become part of the church basketball team, but I have never forgotten that incident. And I can assure you I have never committed another intentional foul.

Oh, yes. Good old number twelve regained consciousness and actually came back to play in that game. But we beat them. Number twelve just wasn't the same after I ran into him. Of course, all of this was revealed to me on the bus ride home, since I missed the rest of the game while I was outside quickly accumulating a layer of ice. And to the best of my recollection, that was the end of my church basketball career.

You may have figured out by now that each story I tell will illustrate an important point in the "Mile Marker" chapter that follows it. But be careful, the part of the story I choose as the illustrative point may surprise you! For example, the obvious application of this basketball experience is the concept of me choosing to do something I knew was wrong. But instead, I want you to focus on something else: those three symbols Teddy and I shared across the gym floor. Jesus used three symbols to illustrate the same three abstract concepts—victory, peace, and hope. Read on and we will discover exactly how He did it.

1

MILE MARKER

VICTORY OVER DESPAIR AND DISCORD

TEACHERS KNOW THAT the best way to explain abstract concepts is through concrete symbols. Jesus was the Master Teacher, who excelled at using stories, miracles, and symbols to explain truth. He communicated abstract concepts through parables ("The kingdom of God is like . . ." [Mark 4:26]), miracles (turning water into wine to illustrate how He can produce a high quality of life—like a fine wine—out of the bland nothingness of water [John 2:1-11]), and symbols ("I am the bread of life" [John 6:35]).

A series of symbols occurred during an event at the end of Christ's public ministry—the Triumphal Entry. You may know it as Palm Sunday, which happens to be the Sunday before Easter. Through that procession into Jerusalem, Jesus was telling us with three powerful symbols—victory, peace, and hope—how we could have triumph over discord and despair. Allow me to set up the story.

THE SETTING

> *"The next day the large crowd who had come to the feast, when they heard that Jesus was coming to Jerusalem . . ."*

JOHN 12:12

If you didn't have the background to this story, that verse would seem to make perfect sense. Jesus, by now a very popular yet controversial figure in and around Jerusalem, was making plans to return to the city to celebrate the upcoming Passover feast. This feast commemorated God protecting His people from the angel of death in Egypt when they marked their doorposts with the blood of a lamb. Good, faithful, religious people wanted to remember that miraculous event. And Jerusalem was the center of their religious universe, so being there made it even better.

That Jesus would go to Jerusalem for Passover makes perfect sense, if you leave out one piece of the story. . . .

Jesus was on the "Most Wanted" list of the Jewish leaders at the exact same time this Passover occurred!

Yes, things were heating up between the religious leaders and Jesus as recorded in the Gospel of John:

Jesus said to them, "Truly, truly, I say to you, before Abraham was born, I am." Therefore they picked up stones to throw at Him, *but Jesus hid Himself and went out of the temple.*

JOHN 8:58-59, *emphasis added*

It didn't matter that Jesus was doing miraculous things, like healing a man who had been blind from birth.

The Jews then did not believe it of him, that he had been blind and had received sight, until they called the parents of the very one who had received his sight, and questioned them, saying, "Is this your son, who you say was born blind? Then how does he now see?" His parents answered them and said, "We know that this is our son, and that he was born blind; but how he now sees, we do not know; or who opened his eyes, we do not know. Ask him; he is of age, he will speak for himself." His parents said this because they were afraid of the Jews; *for the Jews had already agreed that if anyone confessed Him to be Christ, he was to be put out of the synagogue.*

JOHN 9:18-22, *emphasis added*

Once when Jesus was in Jerusalem to observe the Festival of Dedication (Hanukkah), He was stopped and questioned about whether or not He was the Christ, the promised Messiah.

"I and the Father are one." The Jews picked up stones again to stone Him. Jesus answered them, "I showed you many good works from the Father; for which of them are you stoning Me?"

> *The Jews answered Him, "For a good work we do not stone You, but for* blasphemy; *and because You, being a man,* make Yourself out to be God." JOHN 10:30-33, *emphasis added*

Jesus told them He had been sanctified and sent into the world by the Father:

> *"If I do not do the works of My Father, do not believe Me; but if I do them, though you do not believe Me, believe the works, so that you may know and understand that the Father is in Me, and I in the Father." Therefore they were* seeking again to seize Him, *and He eluded their grasp.*
>
> JOHN 10:37-39, *emphasis added*

When reports of Jesus raising Lazarus from the dead got back to the Jewish religious leaders, their fury escalated:

> *Therefore the chief priests and the Pharisees convened a council, and were saying, "What are we doing? For this man is performing many signs.* If we let Him go on like this, all men will believe in Him, *and the Romans will come and take away both our place and our nation." But one of them, Caiaphas, who was high priest that year, . . . prophesied that Jesus was going to die for the nation [of Israel]. . . . So from that day on* they planned together to kill Him.
>
> JOHN 11:47-49, 51, 53, *emphasis added*

It was getting more and more dangerous for Jesus in Jerusalem:

Therefore Jesus no longer continued to walk publicly *among the Jews, but went away from there to the country near the wilderness, into a city called Ephraim; and there He stayed with the disciples. Now the Passover of the Jews was near, and many went up to Jerusalem out of the country before the Passover to purify themselves. So they were seeking for Jesus, and were saying to one another as they stood in the temple, "What do you think; that He will not come to the feast at all?" Now the chief priests and the Pharisees had given orders that if anyone knew where He was, he was to report it,* so that they might seize Him.   JOHN 11:54-57, *emphasis added*

Is it clearer now? Jesus, a man on the run, Jerusalem's Most Wanted, a falsely accused fugitive who was being hunted down for His very life, was so publicly making His grand entrance.

How could Jesus be so "out there" when He was being pursued by people with such violent intentions?

The most succinct answer would be three words. . . . It was Passover.

And most Jews came from far and wide to celebrate this feast in . . . Jerusalem.

This was a huge gathering of people. It was Super Bowl weekend, Mardi Gras, a U2 concert, the circus, Carnivale, and the Boston Marathon all rolled into one event. There is a case to be made that Jesus could have been lost in an extremely large crowd, perceived as just another celebrant.

It also explains why the people could cheer for Him in such a public manner. There was so much yelling and cheering and celebrating going on, perhaps the religious leaders couldn't distinguish one cheering crowd from another.

But more significant even than Christ being there is how he used several of his actions to symbolize even greater truths. Let's look at these symbols.

MAKING SENSE OF THE SYMBOLS

Word had gotten out that Jesus was on His way to Jerusalem:

> *On the next day the large crowd who had come to the feast, when they heard that Jesus was coming to Jerusalem, took* the branches of the palm trees *and went out to meet Him, and* began to shout "Hosanna! *Blessed is He who comes in the name of the Lord, even the King of Israel." Jesus,* finding a young donkey, sat on it; *as it is written, "Fear not, daughter of Zion; behold your King is coming, seated on a donkey's colt."*
>
> JOHN 12:12-15, *emphasis added*

Remember that the best way to teach abstract concepts is through the use of concrete symbols? Even more effective is when the symbols are connected to the senses. The symbols we remember the longest are the ones we can see, hear, taste, touch, or smell.

First, the palm branches. When the people were

strewing the branches in front of Jesus as He was riding into town, it must have been quite a sight. Everyone saw it. But then I started thinking about it more. Have you ever picked up a palm branch? Having lived eleven years in south Florida and now more than twenty years in Southern California, I have encountered a palm branch or two. It may look smooth from a distance, but when you pick one up, you instantly feel its scratchy, rough, prickly texture. You can get an unwanted splinter from a palm branch if you're not careful.

So here was the crowd of people with the palm branches, a symbol that engaged their senses of sight and touch. I wonder if, years later, someone who participated in that day's festivities was outside picking up fallen palm branches after a windstorm—only to be transported back to that memorable day when Jesus came into town.

Second, Jesus rode into town on a donkey. From a sensory perspective, donkeys look distinctly different from horses. When you see those ears, you know it's a donkey. But there's something else. Now, I am essentially a city boy from Philadelphia who had little interaction with live donkeys when I was growing up. (Donkeys of the equine kind, that is.) But I did see donkeys at the zoo or at the county fair and when I visited my friend on his uncle's farm. I know donkeys have a distinct look and a distinct, well, smell.

People who know more than I do about animals assure

me that every animal has a distinct smell. Therefore, there would be an unforgettable donkey smell when Jesus rode by. And, of course, since donkeys were plentiful in first-century Jerusalem, everyone knew that smell. Can't you imagine a person who saw (and smelled) Jesus coming into town that day revisiting the entire spectacle in his mind every time he caught a whiff of the old donkey out back? Once again, a strong symbol!

Third, the crowd's verbal response to the Lord Jesus was symbolic: They shouted "Hosanna!" Have you ever been in the midst of a cheering crowd at a sports event or some other gathering? You look around at the sea of faces in wonder, but more than anything, you remember the sound. The people filling the streets in Jerusalem on that day heard one another sing that song of praise to Jesus.

Three powerful sensory symbols, all included in the account of Jesus' triumphal entry into Jerusalem. Now let's examine what they meant.

WHAT THE SYMBOLS MEANT IN JESUS' DAY

Why did God orchestrate the events of Palm Sunday to unfold the way they did? Some of the events were clear signals of a deeper message. In other words, the symbols truly symbolized more than meets the eye. I can still recall vividly how, as a student at Dallas Seminary, I listened with awe and wonder as the professors explained to me for the first time the meanings behind these symbols.

First, let's look at the palm branches. In the first century, the meaning of those branches was unmistakable. The palms symbolized victory. If the hometown army was off fighting to protect its people, and if that army was, in fact, victorious in defending its cause, the soldiers were met with palm branches as they reentered the town.

Think of it as a first-century ticker-tape parade. You may never have experienced a ticker-tape parade, where the air is filled with a blizzard of confetti. Those kinds of parades often took place when victorious troops returned from World War II, as well as to welcome home the first U.S. astronauts. Today, you might see a sports team honored in their hometown with a modern-day version of this parade to emphasize "No one got the best of us. We won!"

For me, the palms are like the number-one signs that Teddy kept flashing to me during the fateful basketball game. "No one's gonna beat us," he was saying by that hand gesture. "We're number one in the church league. We're only a few minutes away from another victory!"

Second, let's consider the donkey. Why did Jesus choose to ride into town on a donkey? A horse would have been showier, even regal. Or how about Jesus riding in a chariot drawn by magnificent horses? That would have been a display of strength and authority. But a horse signified war, military action, an ongoing battle. That wasn't what

Jesus was about. He came in peace. The people in Jesus' day knew that a donkey represented peace.

In the ticker-tape-parade analogy, it was as if Jesus were riding in the back of a convertible in that parade. It's as if he were saying, "The battle is over, the victory is won. I come to you in peace." In fact, a few chapters after this scene in John's Gospel, the disciple recorded these famous words of Jesus: "Peace I leave with you" (14:27).

Back to my basketball story. The donkey in Jesus' day was a lot like the peace sign I flashed back to Teddy. When the sixties generation first started using the peace sign, our parents thought we were copying Winston Churchill's famous "V for Victory" hand sign. But it wasn't a sign of victory; it was a sign of a life without discord, a sign of peace, a sign that brought a bit of hope and comfort to all of us in those tumultuous times that were a-changin'.

When Jesus rode into Jerusalem on a donkey, He also fulfilled a prophecy made hundreds of years before in the Old Testament. Listen to what the prophet Zechariah said:

> *Rejoice greatly, O daughter of Zion! Shout in triumph, O daughter of Jerusalem! Behold, your king is coming to you; He is just and endowed with salvation, humble, and mounted on a donkey, even on a colt, the foal of a donkey.*
>
> ZECHARIAH 9:9

Third, the people were shouting hosanna. Why were they shouting? And why were they shouting that particular word?

I love the way this series of events came together like a perfect storm. During Passover every year, without fail, the Jewish people were instructed to sing aloud from their book of Psalms. A favorite during Passover was Psalm 118. Near the end is this portion of a verse:

Please LORD, please save us.   PSALM 118:25, NLT

That's how it reads in today's English. But the beauty of this story is that the Jews of the first century would have been singing that psalm in Hebrew, and the phrase "Lord, save us" is summed up in one wonderful Hebrew word: *Hosanna.*

Do you see what's going on here? The people are not in some rebellious state of mind. They are singing exactly as they have been instructed. But they are singing the psalm to Jesus! They are saying to Him, "You are our hero. We need a Messiah. We need a Savior. We need You!" This psalm was sung at every Passover in the hope that the Messiah would come in that generation to save the Jews. "Hosanna" was the sound of hope.

I compare the shouting of hosanna to Teddy's thumbs-up sign in my church basketball league game. It was a sign of hope. "You can do it, Bill," Teddy was saying to me with that thumb pointing to the sky. "I believe in you. Be encouraged."

JESUS' TRIUMPHAL ENTRY IS A TRIUMPH FOR YOU AND ME

Each one of these three symbols adds sensory dimensions to Jesus' arrival in Jerusalem—the palm branches, the donkey, the shouts of hosanna. The symbols define Jesus and His relationship to you and me. Each one of us is victorious because of who Jesus is and what He did.

We don't have to live in defeat. I'm not just talking about a ball game or even a war. I am talking about life itself!

We've all known defeat at some point in our lives, and most of us know how to rise above it. But sometimes it feels as if we're stuck underwater, where everything is slowed down and every step requires incredible effort. Whatever our personal struggle may be—an addiction, a health issue, a broken or struggling relationship—we keep coming back to the question, how can we live in victory?

The apostle John has the answer for us in his first epistle:

> *For whatever is born of God overcomes the world; and this is the victory that has overcome the world—our faith.*
>
> 1 JOHN 5:4

It is our faith that brings us the victory over the circumstances of the world. A man once shared a story with me that illustrates this well. This committed Christian hosts regular meetings specifically for men as a way to reach out to guys with the liberating message of the gospel. At one meeting, he asked the men a simple question: "How many of you participated in high school sports?" Quite a few hands went up. He continued. "Good. Who would like to tell us about one moment of victory that you can recall?"

The room seemed to come alive with excitement. One man remembered being part of the offensive line on his high school football team when they won the league championship his senior year. A former baseball player was proud to be part of a championship baseball team. Even though he wasn't a starter, everyone on the team shared the victorious outcome of a year's hard work. A third man replayed the thrilling moment when he ran in a track-and-field event, achieving both the winning time and his personal best.

All stories of victory. Left at that, these stories aren't all that extraordinary. The extraordinary part is that you wouldn't have guessed that any of these men had ever been victorious in their lives. The host of the meetings was an officer in the Salvation Army, and the men who told their stories of victory were from an inner-city mission run by the organization. In other words, these were stories of victory from men who were homeless.

I literally got goose bumps when I heard this Christian tell me how he explained to the men that, just as they had experienced victory as high school athletes, they could experience triumph through a relationship with Christ. That by believing in Him they could possess the power they needed to overcome the circumstances of their current situations and live a new life in Christ.

You may not be homeless today, but if you are living a defeated life, the message of victory is as available to you as it was to those men in the mission.

First, think about where you already have victory, thanks to your faith in Christ. You have victory over death. You have victory over the sin that constantly tempts you. You have victory over your doubts. You have victory over your worries because God promises He will meet all your needs.

In 2004, after much prayer and preparation, my second wife, Kathi, and I launched a service for people who wanted to improve their public-speaking skills. The Butterworth Communicators Institute was launched with its first three-day seminar, "Finding Your Speaking Voice." Working with fifteen people per session, I felt I could help people—accomplished speakers and absolute novices—raise the level of their speaking ability a few notches higher. Looking back, I believe we have achieved that goal in the lives of the people who have attended our sessions.

But I remember vividly the days leading up to the first event. For some reason, I was overwhelmed with doubts and feelings of defeat. *Do we really need another seminar like this one?* I asked myself cynically. *Do I really think I can help people like I promised I would? So I've been speaking publicly for three decades. Big deal! Who would want to learn from me?* My mind was flooded with lies from the devil himself. And I was allowing myself to believe them.

But God had His way. I got down on my knees with Him the night before the first session. His message to me was crystal clear: Trust Me.

Early in the morning before the conferees arrived, Kathi and I went through the entire seminar room and prayed over each chair, asking God to give the person who would be sitting there a profound experience in the world of public speaking. God answered our prayer. We didn't need to live in defeat. We were given the victory.

There's a second lesson for each of us in the events surrounding the Triumphal Entry: *We don't have to live in discord.* The world around us may be completely scrambled, with strife on every side. We may not know which way is right side up. But we can live with this promise written by the apostle Paul:

> *And the peace of God, which surpasses all comprehension, will guard your hearts and your minds in Christ Jesus.* PHILIPPIANS 4:7

But, you say, what about the people who are facing overwhelming obstacles in life that are creating a wedge between life as they know it and peace as they want it? People who have had the bottom fall out of their lives? Where do they turn when it seems all hope is gone? How can they find peace in circumstances with that level of intensity?

Ruben Guzman is a wonderful example of how to find peace in the midst of peril. A personal friend of mine, Ruben experienced one of those life-shattering blows. Way too early in his young life, Ruben was diagnosed with a horrible disease known as cardiac amyloidosis. He was forty-three years old, and the doctors told him he had only six months to live. He vowed to beat the disease and was extremely aggressive about his treatment, using the best doctors possible at the University of California at San Diego, the University of California at Los Angeles, and the Mayo Clinic. But the most amazing part of Ruben's story is his attitude of joy, peace, and acceptance. As a result of the way he lived, his life was incredibly uplifting to those around him. He was often asked to tell his story in front of groups. This is a taste of some Ruben inspiration:

> On May 17, 2004, I was told by my hematologist that I had contracted a very serious blood disease and that my long-term chance of survival was essentially zero. Over the next few days I spent a lot of time on the Internet researching my disease. The news was almost always very bad. There were survivors out there, but they were few and far between.

When I started giving the news to my family, friends, and coworkers, I discovered something fascinating. God had given me absolute and total peace about what was happening to me. I always knew that God would never abandon me; what I didn't know was that God would shower me with so much of His love that I would walk around with a feeling that God's arms were wrapped around me, comforting me every second of every day. I realized that my disease is an amazing opportunity to share with others just how wonderful a personal relationship with God is.

God also gave me a very personal gift. He gave me a greater and deeper understanding of two words. The first word is tragedy. What's happening to me is not a tragedy; it's a normal part of life. I accepted Jesus Christ as my personal Savior when I was a kid. I placed this physical body into God's hands [knowing] His will would be done. A true tragedy is when a nonbeliever dies.

The second word that God allowed me to understand more clearly is miracle. If I'm cured of this disease, and believe me I really want that to happen, I won't consider it a miracle. My personal miracle occurred long before I was born when my dad accepted Jesus Christ as his personal Savior. That led him to raise a family in which all have accepted Jesus Christ as Savior, and my sisters and I grew up loving the Lord. All the blessings that have followed in my life are a direct result of my dad accepting Christ. Now that's a miracle!

Every day God continues to amaze me. He's brought

*amazingly brilliant and caring doctors into my life. We went to
the Mayo Clinic in Minnesota a few weeks ago, and the doctors
told us about a new treatment protocol that shows great promise for treating my disease. The doctors with the most experience in the world treating this disease had just told me that
I might survive. Trish [my wife] and I were ecstatic, of course.
But this news didn't change anything in my life. Whether I'm
completely cured or whether I live or die is irrelevant to me.
I accept whatever God's plan for my future is—I have peace
about it, and I praise Him for it.*

Watching Ruben live out his peace was a vivid illus-
tration to me of how a person's mind-set can affect him
or her physically. Even though the doctors gave him only
six months to live, Ruben beat that prognosis and lived
for another two years. Sure, it was tough, and Ruben was
human, just like all of us, so he had his strengths and
his weaknesses. But the point is he lived with a constant
attitude of peace, knowing his life could end without
warning.

On June 22, 2006, Ruben went to heaven, the place
of everlasting peace. I gave a eulogy at the service, overwhelmed with how many people had been impacted by
this man's life and his quiet quest for peace.

So just like my friend Ruben, I can live in peace. I can
choose it for myself. I don't have to live in constant strife.
I don't have to live in a place where I have ongoing argu-

ments with myself inside my head. And I don't have to live discontented. No discord for me. I choose peace.

There's a final truth to hang on to: *We don't have to live in despair.* We can live lives that are characterized by hope, not despair. The apostle Peter put it this way:

> *Blessed be the God and Father of our Lord Jesus Christ, who according to His great mercy has caused us to be* born again to a living hope *through the resurrection of Jesus Christ from the dead.* 1 PETER 1:3, *emphasis added*

This is the message that God wants us to hear. In a world characterized by despair, Christ offers us hope. Those of us who know Him know that this is the core of the gospel message. Without the Lord Jesus in our lives, there is nothing to look forward to but despair. Yet Christ brings hope through salvation in Him.

Perhaps you have a relationship with the Lord, but you have allowed the aspect of hope to elude you. Maybe you are a recent victim of an unwanted divorce, and you're having a difficult time seeing any light at the end of the tunnel.

Or perhaps you have just been told by your doctor that you have a serious medical condition. "Where is the hope in that circumstance?" you ask in total candor.

It could be that financial ruin seems to be following you. Or you lie awake at night in your bed, worrying about how your new little baby or grandbaby will be able to survive in today's world.

The possibilities seem depressingly endless, but what is *truly* endless is the hope you have in Christ.

"I came that they may have life, and have it abundantly," Jesus said in John 10:10. He meant it. In Him, you have purpose in your life. In Him, you have strength.

So the next time you're feeling defeated or stressed out or filled with despair, just repeat these three phrases:

I CAN HAVE VICTORY OVER DEFEAT.

I CAN HAVE PEACE OVER DISCORD.

I CAN HAVE HOPE OVER DESPAIR.

TWO

CHAPTER

THE LESSON FROM THE GTO

LOVING WORDS LIKE I do, I find it fascinating to hear how some folks interchange words that are similar in meaning but have just enough nuance of difference that the switch can become bothersome.

Two words that come to mind are *vision* and *focus*. They are similar in meaning, yet the distinction between them makes all the difference in the world. Another story from my youth will illustrate:

Remember my friends Teddy and Bobby? The three of us were inseparable, sort of a Philadelphia version of the Three Musketeers—except when you read this story, you may think the more appropriate nickname is the Three Stooges.

None of us were born into wealthy families, but Teddy's parents seemed to take better care of him financially than most of the other parents did for their kids. So it made perfect sense to us that the day Teddy turned sixteen, his dad drove him down to the driver's facility to get his license and from there to the local dealership to get his first car. And not just any car. No, it was a car any young man would be proud to drive.

It was a brand-new 1968 Pontiac GTO convertible with mag wheels, bucket seats, leather interior, and, of course, it was painted candy apple red.

Teddy promptly left the car lot, heading west on the main highway to pick up Bobby and me for our first test-drive together. My house was the first stop, so I jumped into the passenger seat with unbridled enthusiasm. "This is so cool!" I exclaimed. (It was 1968, so I could have replaced *cool* with *groovy*, but to the best of my recollection I used *cool* to describe it.)

Bobby's house was not much farther away. As we pulled up, he jumped into the backseat with excitement equal to mine.

Off we went, bound for a stretch of road where we knew we could test the GTO's ability to speed. By now the sun had been long gone, but somehow the car still shone like a fireball in the evening sky.

It didn't take long for us to give the car an A+ for speed. She was as fast as had been advertised. At this point in the evening we made the executive, unilateral decision that it was nothing short of criminal to be driving around in a convertible with the top still up.

So the top came down.

Which makes this as good a time as any to tell you that this evening drive around the greater Philadelphia area took place . . .

in February . . .

in the middle of a snowstorm.

Within minutes, the three of us were freezing. Especially Bobby in the backseat. From his vantage point, the idea of a windshield providing protection suddenly seemed revolutionary.

"I'm coming up front with you guys," Bobby announced.

"There's no room," I answered. "They're bucket seats, not a bench seat."

"I don't care. I'll straddle the console. It has to be warmer up there!" Bobby climbed over and got situated. Straddling the console didn't look all that comfortable to me, but Bobby seemed pleased to have the additional protection from the wind.

Then Teddy said, "I think we should have a contest."

This was not an original concept for the three of us. Sometimes it felt as if our entire teenage existence was made up of a series of contests, games, and competitions. Things like who could eat the most at All-You-Can-Eat

Pizza Night at the local pizzeria. Or who could hang from the high dive the longest before his weary arms cramped up and he fell in. Or who could make the most layups before missing the easiest shot in basketball.

No, we were no strangers to contests. But what could Teddy possibly be thinking on this frigid February night in his one-hour-old GTO?

"I suggest we move our rear ends up to the front edge of the seats, so we can stick our heads above the windshield. We can rest our chins on the top of the windshield. I'll drive as fast as I can, and we'll see who can keep his face in the wind the longest."

Teddy smiled while Bobby and I grimaced. This didn't sound like fun. It sounded like torture. *Maybe Teddy's suffering from brain freeze,* I thought.

But when you are a teenage boy, there's very little wiggle room to get an exemption from these contests without your manhood, your family of origin, and a variety of other issues being brought into question. What was amazing was that somehow Teddy always had a valid reason to keep from participating in our contests while still maintaining his dignity.

"Uh-oh," he lamented (but not too much). "If I put *my* head above the windshield, I can't reach the gas pedal with my right foot. I guess you two will have to be the contestants and I'll just do the driving."

How convenient.

But Bobby and I had been through this routine before, and we knew there was no arguing with Teddy. So we quickly moved on to the next part of our debacle. "We need the stating of the contest's rules," Bobby announced, and I nodded in agreement. Whoever won had to win fair and square. No cheating allowed.

"Can you wear a hat?" I asked. Again, it was 1968 and we were all wearing those wool ski caps just like Michael Nesmith on *The Monkees* television show.

"As long as you can keep it on your head," Bobby pronounced, knowing from his recent backseat experience that the wind would blow it right off.

It was at this point that I went to the GTO's glove compartment, which, even though Teddy had owned the car for only an hour, already contained man's best friend . . . a roll of duct tape.

Before anyone could say anything, I began unrolling the duct tape and rolling it onto my head—around the hat, over my right cheek, then my chin, followed by the left cheek, and back over my hat. I did this again and again, ending up with yards of duct tape wrapped around my head. It was clear my hat was going nowhere.

As soon as I put the duct tape down, Bobby picked it up. He wasn't going to be outdone. Bobby imitated my wrapping procedure to the last curve.

It was time for the contest to begin. Bobby and I scooted up as far as we could—me on the seat and Bobby on the console—and solemnly balanced our duct-taped chins on the top of the GTO's windshield. When we both felt comfortable, we gave Teddy the thumbs-up signal (there it is again!) and he peeled out, burning rubber for what seemed like several hundred yards.

The sensation of having my face above the windshield almost defies description. The wind was so fierce, so biting, it literally took my breath away. The icy blast made my eyes tear up, and I began to cry without being able to stop. The temperature was so low that my tears froze into miniscule ice cubelets. And then the wind blew them back, stinging my eyes.

It was like nothing I had ever experienced. Just as my brain was concluding that this was truly one of the most bizarre moments in my life, things got even more interesting. There was a sound, slightly muffled by the duct tape swaddling my head. What was that sound?

Ahh, a police siren. Directly behind us. We were being pulled over.

Bobby and I quickly slid back down in our seats, attempting to regain some sort of decorum before the officer approached the car. Still, I couldn't resist tossing a little barb at Teddy—the guy who always eluded all the danger. After all, he wasn't suffering from a frostbitten face!

"Boy, you're in trouble now," I commented. "Speeding while driving with two duct-taped heads hovering above your windshield. That's tough luck, man."

"You have no idea the trouble I am in," Teddy replied. There was something about his response that made the situation sound more ominous.

"What are you talking about?" I asked.

"My driver's license says I'm supposed to be wearing glasses, and I don't have my glasses with me. He's gonna write me up for that one too." He sounded so sad.

"I wish I could help you," I said in a soft voice as Teddy pulled the car over to the shoulder of the road, awaiting the officer's appearance.

"You can," Teddy suddenly blurted out. Before I could get one word out, Teddy leaned over and ripped the glasses off my face. (Since my glasses were under multiple layers of duct tape, the word *ripped* is painfully and accurately descriptive.)

Now, Teddy's action caused a dual dilemma: Teddy, who didn't need Coke-bottle-thick lenses like mine couldn't see a thing with them, and I couldn't see a thing without them.

"I need your driver's license and vehicle registration," the officer said. I could hear Teddy fumbling around in his wallet. Why was Teddy taking so long? Was he having trouble recognizing his brand-new driver's license without the use of his full eyesight?

"This is a Sears card, son," the policeman said to Teddy. I cringed. *Oh no,* I thought. *He's gonna take us all to prison. I'm going to be doing hard time for criminal use of duct tape on my head. Where's the justice? the righteousness? the grace?*

At this point I think the officer figured out what was going on with the eyeglasses. Suddenly, Bobby, the seeing-eye boy, became the translator too.

"Does your mom know you're out here tonight, son?" the officer asked. When Teddy didn't answer immediately, Bobby jammed one of his elbows into Teddy's ribs.

"No, sir, she doesn't. Please don't tell her, Officer." This time it was me, after a hard crack to the ribs from Bobby, speaking in the general direction I hoped the policeman was located.

We sat in deafening silence as the long arm of the law went back to his patrol car to write us up. Later I learned he only cited Teddy for speeding, but not without one additional comment. "Do you know why I pulled you over?"

"For speeding," Teddy replied.

"No, not really," he paused. "It's because of those two weirdos!" he exclaimed, pointing at Bobby and me.

Perhaps the most frightening part of the entire experience was the policeman's final words: "Okay, boys, you can go now. But I think I will follow you for a little bit to make certain you get on your way okay."

Still wearing my thick glasses, Teddy drove, following Bobby's verbal commands as best he could. ("A little to the left, now keep it straight. Whoops, a little to the right now. Get off the speed bumps, nice and easy. . . .")

A pretty crazy story, wouldn't you agree? But there is a method to my madness in telling it. I wanted you to experience that story in order to understand a key concept we will develop in greater detail in the next chapter. Here it is in a nutshell:

I need more than vision. I need focus.

Teddy and I both had vision, albeit poor vision. His eyesight was better than mine, so when he put on my glasses, everything went blurry. And, of course, when I tried to see without my glasses I had the same experience.

But neither of us could have been described as blind. We had the ability to see, we just needed glasses to help strengthen our eyes. That's where focus comes into the picture. Focus goes a step further than vision. I think of vision as the ability to see, whereas I see focus as the ability to see clearly. Focus involves a little more concentration, a little more effort, and a little less distraction. It is focus that we need for victory over our fears and our doubts. The Lord Jesus knew the power of focus. Let's look at how He demonstrated it to His disciples.

2

MILE MARKER

VICTORY OVER FEAR AND DOUBT

JESUS TAUGHT US much about how focus can bring us victory over issues like doubt and fear. It was a message He gave not only verbally, but symbolically, through His miracles. And no miracle is more vivid in depicting focus over fear than the miracle of Jesus walking on the water. The event is recorded by Matthew, Mark, and John. We will spend most of our time looking at the Matthew account, because it contains the most information. But we will bring in the details, insights, and color commentary from the other Gospels too.

I remember studying the miracles of Christ in seminary. When we came to the miracle of Jesus walking on the water, we were taught that the primary reason this miracle occurred was to teach us that Jesus had power over nature, which is the foundational truth. Human beings don't walk on the top of water. Gravity pulls them down into the sea. But Jesus proved He was more than just a human being. He was the God-man.

But when you look at this one miracle, you discover that the miracle of Jesus walking on the water is accompanied by other miracles in the same context. Jesus walking on the water is not a singular miracle in this circumstance. Actually, I like to think of what happened that night as a miracle times five.

A MIRACLE TIMES FIVE

Let's begin with the obvious:

Jesus walked on the water.

> *Immediately after this, Jesus insisted that his disciples get back into the boat and cross to the other side of the lake, while he sent the people home. After sending them home, he went up into the hills by himself to pray. Night fell while he was there alone.*
>
> *Meanwhile, the disciples were in trouble far away from land, for a strong wind had risen, and they were fighting heavy waves. About three o'clock in the morning Jesus came toward them, walking on the water. When the disciples saw him walking on the water, they were terrified. In their fear, they cried out, "It's a ghost!"*
>
> *But Jesus spoke to them at once. "Don't be afraid," he said. "Take courage. I am here!"*

Then Peter called to him, "Lord, if it's really you, tell me to come to you, walking on the water."

"Yes, come," Jesus said.

So Peter went over the side of the boat and walked on the water toward Jesus. But when he saw the strong wind and the waves, he was terrified and began to sink. "Save me, Lord!" he shouted.

Jesus immediately reached out and grabbed him. "You have so little faith," Jesus said. "Why did you doubt me?"

When they climbed back into the boat, the wind stopped. Then the disciples worshiped him. "You really are the Son of God!" they exclaimed. MATTHEW 14:22-33, NLT

Because Jesus was both fully God and fully man, He could miraculously defy the law of gravity. In other words, don't try this at home, kids, unless you have the full power of God Himself at your disposal!

But Mark, in his Gospel, gives us an insight into another miraculous event that occurred in the midst of this evening at sea:

Jesus walked faster than they could row the boat!

He came to them, walking on the sea; and He intended to pass by them. MARK 6:48

I find this not only miraculous, but rather humorous as well. Mark describes Jesus walking on the water in a rather matter-of-fact way. Oh, yes, Mark says, Jesus was walking on the sea, but what's really cool is that He was power walking at such a brisk pace that His intention was to scurry right by the disciples in the boat and beat them to the other side!

Think about this. You're a disciple and it's the middle of the night. You are rowing a boat after a long, hard day. Then suddenly, you see a figure on top of the water. Are you hallucinating because you're so tired? Okay, you conclude, it's an apparition of some sort, and you're still frightened. Prior to its appearance, you were rowing at a steady but not frantic pace. But along with the ghost comes adrenaline. I can imagine these twelve guys rowing at a world-record pace. These guys were hauling.

But so was Jesus! He not only matched their speed, He passed them. Mark implies that if the Lord hadn't ascertained that there were fears to be quelled, He would have blown right by them in the water and met them on the other side.

There is a third miracle here, as well:

Peter got out of the boat, and walked on the water.

MATTHEW 14:29

We will look at this miracle in more detail as we dig deeper into the story, but suffice it to say, this was another miraculous event that occurred in the midst of four other ones.

Here's another miracle that oftentimes gets overlooked in this amazing account:

Jesus got into the boat and immediately the wind stopped.

Then He got into the boat with them, and the wind stopped; and they were utterly astonished. MARK 6:51

Here again, Mark adds some insight into the basic story provided by Matthew. After Peter finished with his walking-on-the-water experience, he returned to the boat. Jesus got into the boat as well. As soon as Jesus' foot touched the bottom of the boat, the wind miraculously ceased. "But wait," I can hear the skeptic saying, "the wind probably just died down at the same time. It was simply a coincidence." Yet look at how Mark describes the disciples' response—"they were utterly astonished." Is that a typical response if the wind just died down? No, I think that's a normal response if something abnormal occurs—like the miraculous cessation of a terrifying wind.

There's a fifth and final miracle to consider:

Jesus got into the boat and immediately the boat was at land.

They were willing to receive Him into the boat, and immediately the boat was at the land to which they were going.

JOHN 6:21

John weighs in with this fascinating tidbit. Peter finished his late-night water stroll and reentered the boat. Jesus was right behind him. In his Gospel, Mark tells us that upon entering the boat, the blustery wind automatically ceased, and, John adds, not only did the wind stop, but the rowboat suddenly became a speedboat—before they had time to catch their breath, they were on the other side of the sea!

We can learn a great deal about Jesus and His power over nature through this miracle taken at face value. But let's take a closer look at Peter. In studying his part in this story, we can see a pattern developing about how a person should deal with doubts and fears. The key aspect is focus.

PETER'S PATTERN FOR DEALING WITH DOUBT AND FEAR

Rather than relying on some superhuman strategy for dealing with doubts and fears, let's examine the stages the disciples—particularly Peter—went through in the account of Jesus walking on the water.

Fear

> *When the disciples saw Him walking on the sea,* they were terrified, *and said "It is a ghost!" And they cried out in fear.* MATTHEW 14:26, *emphasis added*

The circumstances of life can cause anxiety. All of us carry around certain fears that cause us heartache and pain on every level.

Several years ago I wrote about my failed marriage in a book called *New Life after Divorce*. When the book was released, I was unprepared for the number of e-mails and letters I received from fellow strugglers—those who knew the fears, the tears, and the pain of that particular trauma. Everyone told me their personal story, but one sentence in one particular letter captured the sentiment of them all:

I didn't think I would ever get past the pain of my divorce, but you have demonstrated that, after time, healing can occur. Thank you for helping me see that my fears were unfounded.

Fear falls into the three tenses of our lives. For some of us, our greatest fears are fears from our *past*. Such fear has been reduced these days to clichés like "my baggage" or "my stuff" or "my secrets." Everyone who has these fears knows what I'm talking about. It's those issues that frighten you because you would be humiliated beyond belief if those secrets from your past were made known.

Others of us live with the fear of our *present*. We are paralyzed by a set of current circumstances weighing us down right now. Maybe it's fear of a person, or the fear of failure, or the fear of being unable to fight a medical situation. Whatever the specifics, it's real and it's in your face every day.

Finally, others of us struggle with a fear about our *future*. That big word that sends chills down our spine is the word *uncertainty*. Hopefully, your eternal future is settled and not an issue of uncertainty because you understand that when

Mountain in My Rearview Mirror

Jesus died on the cross, He died to pay for all our baggage, all our stuff, all our secrets. Because we put our trust in Him, He has wiped the slate clean and forgiven us of all our shortcomings.

But I'm thinking of uncertainties tied to this life on earth. Issues like, how long will I have to work before I can afford to retire? Will I ever be able to retire? What about my health? Will I be able to live comfortably on a fixed income?

The apostle Paul knew about fear. Read his honest and vulnerable words written to the Corinthian believers (and all believers after):

> *For even when we came into Macedonia our flesh had no rest, but we* were afflicted on every side: conflicts without, fears within. *But God, who comforts the depressed, comforted us by the coming of Titus.*   2 CORINTHIANS 7:5-6, *emphasis added*

The Old Testament has a lot to say about fear as well. Consider this proverb:

> The fear of man brings a snare, *but he who trusts in the LORD will be exalted.*   PROVERBS 29:25, *emphasis added*

Somehow we have to get beyond our fears. Notice what Jesus prescribed as the beginning of the antidote.

Fortitude

> *But immediately Jesus spoke to them, saying,* "Take courage, *it is I; do not be afraid.*   MATTHEW 14:27, *emphasis added*

My response to fear and anxiety should be to stand firm. *Fortitude* is another word for courage. The only way to defeat fear is to face it, stare it down, and have courage enough to stand firm until it goes away.

That is easy to say but hard to live out. More than any other generation, it appears that baby boomers have worked extra hard at looking strong, all put together, and in control, while on the inside we are weak, all messed up, and scared to death.

The courage and the fortitude that we need come from the inside. We're not talking about false bravado here; we're talking about real-live, honest-to-goodness "guts."

Lately, as I've been rereading the Old Testament, I've been impressed all over again with the repetitive use of the words *stand firm*. The answer to our fears is not as simple as turning everything over to God and passively walking away. No, we have a part to play as well. That's why the Lord has words of encouragement like these in His Scriptures:

> *Only* be strong and very courageous; *be careful to do according to all the law which Moses My servant commanded you; do not turn from it to the right or to the left, so that you may have success wherever you go.* JOSHUA 1:7, *emphasis added*

> *Wait for the LORD;* be strong *and* let your heart take courage. PSALM 27:14, *emphasis added*

But this story is far from over. Fortitude is just the beginning of the strategy for defeating the fears that threaten to control our lives. The next step is the real key.

Focus

And He said, "Come!" And Peter got out of the boat, and walked on the water and came toward Jesus.

MATTHEW 14:29, *emphasis added*

Remember the story from the last chapter about Teddy and me and my glasses? When Teddy put on my glasses, he completely lost his ability to focus. And when I didn't have my glasses on, the world was a blurry mess as well. The lesson is simple:

I need more than vision. I need focus. It's more than just the ability to see—it's the ability to see well.

How about another way to put it? I need more than a casual glance; I need an intentional zooming in. I have vision without my glasses on. The world doesn't go black. But when I put my glasses on, I move from vision to focus.

The spiritual lesson here is clear. God is interested in more than an occasional glance. He wants to be our total focus. Think about it in terms of the account of Peter's predicament out on the water.

I love Peter. He is my favorite New Testament character, bar none. The best description I ever heard for Peter is the apostle with the "foot-shaped mouth." I like to think of him as the New Testament version of Homer Simpson.

He had such an uncanny ability to get into messy situations. And this mess on the lake is a classic.

The disciples have been told by the Lord to take courage and not to be afraid. In my mind's eye, I see the twelve obeying the Lord and reaching a place where they could be a little less stressed and a little more relaxed.

I think I'll press this issue a little further, Peter thinks to himself, probably with a wry smile on his weathered face. "Lord, if that is really You, prove it to us by inviting me to join You out there!" I can just see Peter turning to the other eleven and winking at them, as if to say, "I think I just placed one out there for our Lord!"

But of course Jesus, the Master of the understated response, simply replies, "Come."

Now I see eleven guys looking at Peter with an expression that says, "You idiot! We could have told you . . . you don't set one out there for Jesus and think you'll get the better of Him. Just how stupid are you, anyway?"

And this is where I envision Peter mumbling under his breath Homer's famous lament, "D'oh!"

But you have to give Peter credit; he didn't blow off the Lord's invitation. He got out of the boat. And miraculously, he began to walk on the water. How was he able to do that?

Well, the text offers no insight, so allow this drama to unfold in your imagination. As a matter of fact, pretend that you are Peter in this situation. How would you pull it off?

I know how I would. Once I was out of that boat, I would immediately think the following: *People don't walk on the water. It just doesn't happen. But the Lord is doing it. I don't know how He's making it work, but I do know one thing . . . whatever it is that He is doing, I am going to do the same thing!*

Assuming that Peter had similar thoughts, he was able to zoom in on Jesus and His actions. Whatever Jesus did, Peter did.

That's focus!

If Jesus walked on His tiptoes, Peter walked on his tiptoes. If Jesus extended His arms like He was going to fly, Peter did the same. If your theology allows for some humor, you can imagine that this would have been a situation ripe for a laugh or two. Jesus, knowing that Peter was copying Him precisely, could have added a few gestures, gyrations, or superfluous movements to the choreography just to get the laugh!

The point is that Peter gave our Lord more than a casual glance. He was absolutely focused on Him. I think that's why the text says Peter came toward Jesus. Focus made him a copycat.

You know about focus. We all do. It's what we give to God when our lives are upside down, right? It's the prayer that says, "Dear God, I am Yours completely. I will do whatever You want me to do. Especially right now, Lord. If You could just help me get rid of [fill in your own specific overwhelming obstacle], I promise I will serve You faithfully. Really. I will do whatever. If You want me to go to Africa and be a missionary and eat monkey brains, I will do it. Just help me, Lord."

God's Word is full of exhortations to keep our eyes focused on Him. Two of my favorite passages are in Hebrews and in Colossians:

> *Therefore, since we have so great a cloud of witnesses surrounding us, let us also lay aside every encumbrance and the sin which so easily entangles us, and let us run with endurance the race that is set before us,* fixing our eyes on Jesus.
>
> HEBREWS 12:1-2, *emphasis added*

> Set your mind on the things above, *not on the things that are on earth.*   COLOSSIANS 3:2, *emphasis added*

I like to compare people focusing on the Lord to athletes who are "in the zone." It's that sweet spot where all other distractions are eliminated in a concentrated effort to play the game wholeheartedly. The opposing fans' taunts, the opposition's trash-talking, the weather—all are circumstances that get banished from the athlete's mind because his or her performance in the game is all that matters.

In the zone—wouldn't it be great if we could live that way in a spiritual sense? Everything else in life would be secondary compared to our absolute need to stay focused on God!

It's all about looking to the Lord for daily direction in

our lives. It's so simple, so basic. But even though we've all experienced it, we also have all experienced what happened to Peter next.

Forgetting

But seeing the wind . . .   MATTHEW 14:30

It happens to all of us after a period of time when God has answered our prayers. You know what I mean—He has actually delivered us from the dilemma for which we asked help. We get used to life being good again. And we also forget that the reason it is good again is because we had our priorities straight. We were focusing on Jesus. But, pardon my grammar, the gooder it gets, the less likely we are to stay focused. We look away. There's still an occasional glance, but it's nothing like the concentrated focus we exhibited when we needed help.

The same thing happened with Peter. He allowed himself to get distracted. The text says that Peter was "seeing the wind." If Peter was still in a place where he was absolutely focused on the Lord, how could he have seen the wind? He lost his concentration, his focus. He allowed something to distract him. He forgot about how important it was to stay focused.

There will always be distractions that tempt us to take our eyes off what is important—things like health issues, broken relationships, job stress, or even the high winds and waves of a natural disaster. Before you beat yourself up too much over this point, I must add that being distracted appears to be an inbred part of our human nature. All of us develop some level of SADD (spiritual attention deficit disorder).

One of the most profound examples of this dilemma in the Scriptures is recounted in the Pentateuch. The children of Israel had successfully navigated all the overwhelming obstacles that developed between them and the Land of Promise. But God knew that once they arrived there, it would be so easy to lose focus, to become distracted, to forget. The Lord admonished the children of Israel through the words of Moses:

> *For the LORD your God is bringing you into a good land, a land of brooks of water, of fountains and springs, flowing forth in valleys and hills; . . . a land where you will eat food without scarcity, in which you will not lack anything; . . .* Beware that you do not forget the LORD your God *by not keeping His commandments and His ordinances and His statutes which I am commanding you today; otherwise, when you have eaten and are satisfied, and have built good houses and lived in them, . . . then your heart will become proud and* you will forget the LORD your God *who brought you out from the land of Egypt, out of the house of slavery.*
>
> DEUTERONOMY 8:7, 9, 11-12, 14, *emphasis added*

So we all have the same tendency to lose our focus and forget what and who are really important. But there's another problem too.

Fear Again

He became frightened.   MATTHEW 14:30

When we dwell on life's circumstances, anxiety and fear return. Do you see what happened to Peter? He lost all the momentum he had and returned to where he had begun—full of fear!

To be fair to Peter, I am sure it was quite a tempestuous set of circumstances. Apparently, the wind had whipped itself up into quite a frenzy. It was serious enough to catch Peter's attention. It was a strong enough distraction to get him to look away from what was preeminently important—Jesus.

So Peter turned his glance away from the Lord—mistake number one. Mistake number two was allowing the circumstances to overwhelm him. Once again he became afraid. I imagine his stomach tightened up. I can feel that old sense of anxiety returning with its accompanying acid-reflux churning.

Jesus understands that feeling of anxiety. That is why He encouraged us with these familiar words from His famous Sermon on the Mount:

> Do not worry *then, saying, "What will we eat?" or "What will we drink?" or "What will we wear for clothing?" For . . . your heavenly Father knows that you need all these things. But seek first His kingdom and His righteousness, and all these things will be added to you. So* do not worry *about tomorrow; for tomorrow will care for itself.*   MATTHEW 6:31-34, *emphasis added*

Not only had Peter heard Jesus when He preached those words, it looks as if he may have learned the lesson from a firsthand demonstration on the surface of the sea. Years later, he would write these words of encouragement:

> Give all your worries and cares to God, *for he cares about you.* 1 PETER 5:7, NLT, *emphasis added*

The apostle Paul jumps on the anti-anxiety bandwagon as well with these words:

> Be anxious for nothing, *but in everything by prayer and supplication with thanksgiving let your requests be made known to God.* PHILIPPIANS 4:6, *emphasis added*

This verse may be the most helpful because of its simple formula. Don't be anxious. Instead, take all the time and effort normally expended on anxiety and replace it with prayer. Don't worry about anything; instead, pray about everything!

It is important to remember the value of staying focused. In Peter's predicament, losing his focus was caused by forgetting, which led to fear. Let's see from the text how Jesus viewed it.

Faithlessness

> *Immediately Jesus stretched out His hand and took hold of him, and said to him,* "You of little faith, *why did you doubt?"* MATTHEW 14:31, *emphasis added*

Jesus didn't let Peter off the hook. "Why didn't you have the good sense to continue to trust Me?" Jesus seems to be saying. "Why did you allow worry and doubt to reenter the picture?"

Not much faith.

Doubt is such a dastardly thing. When we are at our best, doubt seems to disappear. But in all other circumstances, doubt is there, either filling our minds or ominously lurking in the shadows, ready to rear its ugly head. "You can't do it," doubt tells us. Or even worse, "God can't do it."

Peter must have allowed doubt to creep into his psyche, or else the Lord wouldn't have accused him of his faithless condition.

Why do we worry? Why do we have doubts? In this context the answer is simple:

Worry and doubt are signs that we have lost our focus.

On our own, we worry. We allow distractions to have their way with us. It won't be our shining moment, spiritually speaking. It will be just the opposite. In God's eyes we will appear quite faithless. *But I do have faith,* we want to rebut, yet we feel ashamed that God would think of us in these terms.

But there is an answer: Through focus, trust, and courage, we will succeed.

It all boils down to our faith. Let the familiar words from the book of Hebrews infiltrate your soul:

> *And* without faith it is impossible to please Him, *for he who comes to God must believe that He is and that He is a rewarder of those who seek Him.* HEBREWS 11:6, *emphasis added*

It is fairly obvious that the answer to faithlessness is faith. And that is exactly how Peter's story concludes.

Faith

> *And those who were in the boat worshiped Him, saying,* "You are certainly God's Son!" MATTHEW 14:33, *emphasis added*

This is a profound moment. I see it as a turning point in the lives of the disciples. "You are more than a ghost!" they seem to say. "You are more than a special effect created by a movie studio. You are the Son of God. I believe in You!"

In many ways, focus and faith are synonymous. The familiar words of the apostle Paul come to mind:

> *For we walk by faith, not by sight.* 2 CORINTHIANS 5:7

For our purposes, perhaps we could paraphrase it this way:

> *For we walk by focus, not by vision.*

In the end, it's not what we can see, but how faithful we are to trust God. Seeing only complicates the situation. For what we see often is perceived as opposite of what God should be doing. *How can you allow this evil to prevail in my life, God?* we silently shout in our spirit. *You should be zapping all these difficult things out of my life!* we conclude. Yet if we don't experience immediate relief from hardship, we begin to doubt that God really cares. And nothing could be further from the truth.

To overcome this, you may need to put an action plan into place. Taking the first step means facing your issues. Exactly what are the circumstances that are creating doubt and fear in your life? Don't hurry through this evaluation process. Take some time to seriously reflect on this.

Finding the help you need is the next step. Chances are these overwhelming obstacles are bigger than you can handle on your own. This is where assistance is crucial. I am being purposely nebulous at this point because the type of help you need really depends on how severe the circumstances are. Some situations can be facilitated by a group of close friends. I am a big believer in small groups, accountability partners, mentors, and the like. I know for a fact that many of the issues I have dealt with in life have been made more endurable and more understandable because of caring friends who have walked the path with me.

But I also know that there are many obstacles that are over my head, and the only way to deal with them effectively is through the help of a competent counselor. A professional knows how to help because a professional knows the right questions to ask. To this day I am still grateful to the counselors who have helped me along my way, especially during the times of deepest struggle.

The final step takes us back to where this chapter began: focus on the Lord and His Word. Notice how I phrased that last sentence. I am not asking you to do something impractical like stare blankly at a statue of the Lord Jesus at an old church. The way to focus on the Lord is to focus on His Word. Ask yourself, *What is God saying to me about my situation through the pages of His Scripture? How can I apply the teachings of the Bible to my everyday life? How does a story like Peter's encounter with the Lord out on the water relate to the overwhelming obstacle I am currently experiencing?* Questions like these will get you closer to the answers.

Make the answers a more permanent part of your life by writing them down. Journaling has been one of the most valuable disciplines I have ever developed in my life. I can look back in my journals to see how God has answered my prayers in a variety of situations.

So for now, let these three sentences bring you closer to the answer to your fear and doubt:

- Be certain: Fortitude is the answer to fear.
- Be careful: Forgetting will take you back to fear.
- Be comforted: Faith is a matter of focus.

THREE

CHAPTER

THE LESSON FROM THE BENNY BURKE INCIDENT

IT BECAME KNOWN as the Benny Burke incident. It took place in a small blue-collar town just outside of Philadelphia known as Ambler. I couldn't have been more than five or six years old. Benny lived right down the street from me, off Overlook Road, close to Hayward Road.

It was the late 1950s, that innocent time in a little boy's life when the whole world revolved around one thing . . .

baseball.

It was the time when young boys begged for their own portable transistor radios, each about the size of a box of Altoids, complete with the essential upgrade—an ear-piece to help them get lost in their own world of baseball bliss. Of course, if you were in Ambler, Pennsylvania, the whole world revolved around the Philadelphia Phillies. Any Phillies baseball fan will tell you that the end of the fifties was not the best time in the franchise's history to be a rabid fan.

Still my friends and I would spend hours during baseball season listening to every Phillies pitch, catch, swing, hit, and/or miss. It was sheer delight to listen to the velvety voice of Byrum Saam with the play-by-play, with color commentary provided by Bill Campbell and the former Phillies great Richie Ashburn. There was a rumor going around when I was a kid that Richie Ashburn lived near our little town of Ambler, which made the connection even sweeter.

Yes, when you're six, the universe revolves around your hometown team. Right up there, next to listening to the game on your transistor radio, was the art of collecting baseball cards. When I was a boy in Ambler, there was only one brand—Topps. Each pack contained five cards and a thin strip of pink bubble gum that was harder than a piece of brick. It was all wrapped up in a waxy paper, bargain priced at a nickel a pack.

Every week, once we received our allowance, we would faithfully march down to the little corner store close to downtown Ambler to buy our packs of baseball cards.

We would anxiously rip open the pack, focused on one thing—finding as many Philadelphia Phillies player cards as we could. Since the Phillies were not doing very well, this was a greater challenge than you'd think. We'd routinely see a lot of Yankees and a lot of Dodgers and even a lot of St. Louis Cardinals, but alas the Phillies were not well represented in the packs.

It was this lack of a Phillies card that led Benny Burke to suggest a rather desperate measure one spring afternoon. We had finished a hard day in first grade, slaving over block letters and the tricky world of subtraction.

"How much money do you have?" Benny asked me with a curious tone in his voice.

"I'm broke," I replied honestly. "I spent everything I had on cards yesterday."

"We've got to get more baseball cards," he lamented.

"Well, I don't get my allowance for another five days, so don't look at me. Do you have any money?"

"No," he mumbled, "but I have an idea of how we can get more baseball cards than we've ever had—without spending a lot of money."

"You do?" I asked with splendid naïveté. "What's your idea?"

"We're gonna go down to the five-and-dime and we're gonna steal them."

"Steal them?" I was shocked to my very core. As a faithful member of the First Presbyterian Church of

Ambler, I knew the Twenty-third Psalm by heart, not to mention the less-memorized One Hundreth Psalm. I had been presented with a Bible for perfect attendance—and not just any Bible. It was white—signifying purity—and it had a gold zipper to close it, signifying the importance of taking all wayward and sinful thoughts and shutting them out of your head, much like zipping up your Bible.

Stealing? It was out of the question. Even if it was possible to accomplish the theft without being caught, the guilt alone would eat away my insides like a daily dose of battery acid.

But we were talking about baseball cards—lots of baseball cards. Satan caused visions of Phillies to dance in my head.

"Exactly how would we do it?" I asked, which proved to be my fatal mistake—I showed interest. Benny jumped on it like a used-car salesman.

"We'll walk into the five-and-dime—it's a much bigger store than the corner store, so no one will be looking. When we are convinced the coast is clear, we'll grab the loot and get out of there!"

"But where will we put the cards so that no one sees us?" I asked innocently.

"That's where you come in, buddy," he said with an evil grin. "We will jam the packs of cards down your shorts."

Suddenly it all became clear to me. Benny, who was

as skinny as a hoe handle, wanted me for one reason and one reason only—I was fat. In those days little fat kids wore elastic shorts, so he was imagining a treasure trove of baseball cards conveniently stashed between my elastic shorts and my elastic tighty-whitics. He didn't say it, but he didn't have to—since I was so fat, no one would ever notice the extra bulges surrounding my torso.

"I don't know, Benny," I began to backpedal, the Protestant guilt resurfacing.

"Come on, Billy, don't be a sissy," he chided.

I hated being called a sissy. It was the ultimate put-down in our first-grade class.

"You can do it," he prompted.

And so I did.

It's hard to know what possessed an overweight, Phillies-loving son of a blue-collar railroad man to gather the personal strength to go against everything he knew to be right, but before I knew it, I was in the toy aisle of the five-and-dime. Bobby was down the aisle toward the front of the store, making sure the lady at the checkout counter was sufficiently occupied with other tasks. We waited for what seemed to be an hour and finally Benny gave me the high sign. "Go for it!" he whispered.

With reckless abandon, I began stuffing packs of base-ball cards down my shorts. God had given me these rolls of fat with convenient little pocketlike dips to keep the cards from falling through the leg holes of my shorts. In less than a minute, I was packed to the gills. I had enough cards down my shorts to represent every player in Major League Baseball.

Benny and I knew it was important to maintain a leisurely pace as we exited the store. We didn't want to draw attention to ourselves by sprinting, which is what I felt like doing, even though I had never sprinted before in my life. We sauntered past the lady at the counter, who never even looked up. Soon we would be free men on the mean streets of downtown Ambler!

It was exhilarating beyond description to breathe the fresh air outside the store. We did it! And we didn't get caught! There was no such thing as a "high five" back then or we would have exchanged them. But then, just as Benny and I were about to unload the booty, our world came crashing down.

"Boys! Just a minute, you two. Stop right where you are!"

Benny and I turned around. We were face-to-face with the store's manager. Benny looked at me with an expression that said, *Nuts, I completely forgot about the manager!* Thanks, Benny. Some friend. You are part devil and part moron.

"Come with me," the manager instructed. Both of us were frozen with fear, so we felt our only course of action was to follow him in contrite obedience.

"We had a 482 in the toy aisle," the manager announced

to the checkout lady. She looked us over, clucked her tongue, and shook her head in disgust.

"Ask them if they listen to a lot of Elvis," she muttered. Adults blamed all bad behavior back then on poor old Elvis. But Elvis didn't come up in our conversation. The manager marched us to the back of the store, right into his office.

"What's in your pants, young man?" the manager asked me.

I sat in silence, thinking if I didn't answer, that would be the end of it. After all, it was a rather rude question.

"Take those things out of your pants right now," he commanded. I sadly obeyed. As I pulled them out, packs of baseball cards covered his desk completely, and the overflow fell onto the floor. Even I was amazed at how many packs I had put away in my shorts. It looked as if I had robbed the Topps factory of its complete inventory.

"We're sorry, sir," Benny chimed in with a preemptive apology, made in hopes that we would laugh about this as three men would do and then be on our merry way.

"It's a little late for that," the manager replied.

"So . . . what are you gonna do to us?" Benny asked meekly.

"Well, what I should do is call the police," he answered. At the very mention of the word *police* Benny and I tightened up like a rope full of knots. Thoughts of jail—no, make that thoughts of prison—filled our overactive six-year-old minds. Doing hard time with grown men who would make fun of us sounded like punishment too difficult to bear.

"What do you think?" the manager said. "Should I call the cops on you?"

"No, sir, we've learned our lesson," said Benny. "We will never do anything like this ever again. We promise."

He thought this over for an extensive amount of time. Finally he looked us each straight in the eye and said, "All right, I am going to let you go this time. But I want you both to go straight home and tell your parents what you did. Is that clear?"

"Yes, sir," we replied in unison.

"All right, you can leave."

We ran out of there as fast as our skinny little legs and fat little legs (respectively) would take us.

As soon as we were outside, Benny, the six-year-old hard-core cynic, said, "Tell my parents? Are you kidding? There's no way in the world I am going to tell my parents!"

Just one more act of disobedience by Benny Burke. Yet down deep inside, I knew he had a point. For me, telling my parents about my life of crime made hard time at the prison look like an afternoon with Captain Kangaroo.

That night at the dinner table, I was uncharacteristically quiet. "Everything all right, pal?" my dad asked, sensing something was amiss. On a normal evening I possessed an uncanny ability to chatter like a magpie, while at the same time putting away large quantities of food in record time. That evening the guilt was so intense, not only was I silent, but I was eating only normal portions.

"I'm okay," I muttered in a thoroughly unconvincing way.

"Are you sure?"

"Uh-huh."

"Here are some more potatoes," my mother offered in her usual gesture of love—comfort foods.

I reluctantly agreed to her offer but found out soon enough that even Mom's mashed potatoes couldn't extinguish the burning flame of guilt.

I tried to go through the motions of a normal evening at the house. After dinner, I took my bath, jumped into my pajamas, and joined my parents for a bowl of vanilla ice cream with chocolate syrup in front of the Philco black-and-white television set tuned to a new episode of *The Adventures of Ozzie and Harriet.*

Oh, I thought, *I wish I had the malt shop to go to like David and Ricky did—a place where everything that had gone wrong for them was made right.*

But there was nothing like that in my life on that evening. Soon Ricky Nelson was singing a song, so I knew the episode was almost over. I made my way to the bathroom to brush my teeth, then I went up the stairs for bed. Mom and Dad followed me into my bedroom, listened as I said my prayers (a recitation of the Lord's Prayer), and after tucking me in, they turned off the light and went back downstairs.

As I lay in my bed, surrounded by nothing but utter darkness, I tried my best to be brave. But one can only keep things bottled up for so long.

Before I knew it, I was crying. Quietly at first, but then it turned to weeping. Before long, that was followed by deep, guttural moaning. Whatever my folks were watching on the Philco, the sound of their son sobbing drowned it out. I don't know how they decided who should come up to comfort me, but my dad was soon at my bedside.

"What's the matter, pal?" (He always called me pal.)

"Daddy, I got into big trouble today," I blurted out.

"What did you do?"

And with that, I spilled the whole Benny Burke incident in graphic, emotional detail. I remember being so upset and crying so violently that I could barely get the story out.

Dad had a variety of reactions. He smiled when he heard the part about me stuffing packs of cards down my pants. He scowled when the manager mentioned the police. He looked stern every time I said the name Benny Burke.

But most of all, he just listened. He put his arm around my shoulder. He said it was all going to be okay and that I shouldn't be worried about it anymore. Best of all, he said all was forgiven.

In some ways it is like this episode occurred only yesterday. I say that because I can still remember in vivid detail how upset I was, coupled with how kind, understanding, and forgiving my father was. I think he probably went down the stairs after consoling me, recounted the story to my mother, and ended with a classic line like, "I've never seen him so upset before, so I didn't think I needed to punish him. He's had more than enough punishment for his crime."

Guilt has a way of dealing with us all, doesn't it?

3

MILE MARKER

VICTORY OVER GUILT AND SHAME

AS I AM WRITING these words, an intriguing story in the sports pages has caught my eye. Without mentioning any names, it appears that there is a member of the Los Angeles Lakers professional basketball team who has had a bit of a Benny Burke incident in his own life.

Midway through the regular season, the NBA takes a few days off for the All-Star Game. Those who are good enough to be invited to this game participate in some whirlwind activities. Meanwhile, the players who are not good enough to be considered all-star material are given a week off to rest their bodies and heal from any injuries they might have.

It appears that the aforementioned Laker chose to spend his off week at a popular ski resort in Utah. So far, so good. But of course, it is written into each player's contract that he will do nothing off the court to put his body in danger of injury—in this case, no snow skiing or snowboarding.

At the end of the all-star break, the players return to their teams for the first practice before resuming the season. Our "snow bunny" shows up with a shoulder injury that is serious enough to keep him out of the lineup.

How did he sustain this injury, you ask?

That's what everyone wanted to know, including his coach, Phil Jackson. The initial report was that this player had taken a bad spill on a patch of ice. He claimed that it was black ice, and because he was walking with his hands in his pockets, he was unable to brace himself when he fell, thus the serious shoulder injury.

Sound suspicious to you? Join the club.

"All I can do is take his word," Coach Jackson told the press.

Well, I don't know exactly what happened next, but it is my conclusion that at dinner that evening, our player didn't eat well, even though the cook brought extra potatoes. He asked to be dismissed from the table and promptly headed off upstairs to his room. After watching a little television and having a bowl of ice cream, he went to bed. Apparently the guilt from the whole issue got the best of our Laker, because his crying was loud enough to bring Phil Jackson upstairs to see what was creating all of the ruckus. It must have been at this point that the player confessed that he had, in fact, been on the slopes and that was how he injured his shoulder.

This isn't exactly how it was recounted to the press the next day, but having lived through a similar situation, this is my best guess as to how it all went down.

Why?

The guilt from being dishonest was eating him up.

So whether the issue is stealing baseball cards as a first grader or telling whoppers to your coach as an adult, guilt is something we know when we feel it. I think we can agree that its effects can be classified as an overwhelming obstacle.

Let's begin to unwrap guilt and its complexities by asking a few questions.

WHY DO I FEEL GUILTY?

I can think of at least three reasons why you and I struggle with feelings of guilt. The first reason is *because of something we have done.* In the Benny Burke incident, the reason is quite apparent—I stole the baseball cards!

Yet there's a second reason we can see embedded in that story too. We sometimes feel guilty *because of choices we have made.* It wasn't just that I had stolen the baseball cards. I also felt guilty because I had chosen to join forces with Benny. What a foolish choice I had made!

There's a third reason to note. We may feel guilty *because we could have changed our choice.* I could have walked away! I should have walked away! If I had done what I knew to be right, this whole affair would never have occurred.

Have any of these feelings ever crept into your life? I'm certain the answer is yes. All of us have struggled with feelings of guilt and shame. Even biblical characters were not immune from those raw emotions. Perhaps one of the most famous descriptions of raw guilt revolves around an otherwise amazing man. King David was an admirable man on most counts, but he had his own demons to deal with.

In Psalm 51 we see an exposé of a man laid bare, with only his feelings of guilt as a covering. But before we explore his statement to the police or his confessional, let's lay out some of the background to this part of David's life to help explain more cogently the mess he allowed himself to get into.

> *Then it happened in the spring, at the time when kings go out to battle, that David sent Joab and his servants with him and all Israel, and they destroyed the sons of Ammon and besieged Rabbah. But David stayed at Jerusalem.*

Now when evening came David arose from his bed and walked around on the roof of the king's house, and from the roof he saw a woman bathing; and the woman was very beautiful in appearance.

So David sent and inquired about the woman. And one said, "Is this not Bathsheba, the daughter of Eliam, the wife of Uriah the Hittite?"

David sent messengers and took her, and when she came to him, he lay with her; and when she had purified herself from her uncleanness, she returned to her house.

The woman conceived; and she sent and told David, and said, "I am pregnant."

Then David sent to Joab, saying, "Send me Uriah the Hittite." So Joab sent Uriah to David.

When Uriah came to him, David asked concerning the welfare of Joab and the people and the state of the war.

Then David said to Uriah, "Go down to your house, and wash your feet." And Uriah went out of the king's house, and a present from the king was sent out after him.

But Uriah slept at the door of the king's house with all the servants of his lord, and did not go down to his house.

Now when they told David, saying, "Uriah did not go down to his house," David said to Uriah, "Have you not come from a journey? Why did you not go down to your house?"

And Uriah said to David, "The ark and Israel and Judah are staying in temporary shelters, and my lord Joab and the servants of my lord are camping in the open field. Shall I then go to my house to eat and to drink and to lie with my wife? By your life and the life of your soul, I will not do this thing."

Then David said to Uriah, "Stay here today also, and tomorrow I will let you go." So Uriah remained in Jerusalem that day and the next.

Now David called him, and he ate and drank before him, and he made him drunk; and in the evening he went out to lie on his bed with his lord's servants, but he did not go down to his house.

Now in the morning David wrote a letter to Joab and sent it by the hand of Uriah.

He had written in the letter, saying, "Place Uriah in the front line of the fiercest battle and withdraw from him, so that he may be struck down and die."

So it was as Joab kept watch on the city, that he put Uriah at the place where he knew there were valiant men.

The men of the city went out and fought against Joab, and some of the people among David's servants fell; and Uriah the Hittite also died.   2 SAMUEL 11:1-17

WHY DID DAVID FEEL GUILTY?

Second Samuel 11 reads like an Old Testament version of *Law & Order*!

In Psalm 51 we will see King David pour out his need for forgiveness, based on all the guilt that was stored up in his heart. But now, because of the historical passage we just read, we can explore the question: Why did David feel guilty?

David felt guilty because of murder. The Bible is clear: David was responsible for the murder of Uriah because he instructed Uriah's commanding officer, Joab, to put Uriah in the most dangerous position possible. Uriah's death was all but guaranteed. Most of us don't possess that kind of life-or-death power, but still, we can identify with the guilt. Now the plot thickens: Why did David have to commit murder? The answer reveals the second reason why King David experienced guilt.

David felt guilty because of adultery. The passage begins with one of the most famous stories in the Bible: David sees Bathsheba bathing on her rooftop and lusts for her. Once again, because of his power, David was able to simply have her brought to his residence, where he fulfilled his lustful thoughts by turning them into actions. This single act of adultery burned in his heart like a firebrand. So our *Law & Order* detectives have determined that a murder was committed and that the motive behind the murder was to hide the adultery. But why did David commit adultery in the first place? I believe the text gives us the answer—the third reason why King David felt such strong guilt over all this mess he had created.

David felt guilty because he was in the wrong place at the wrong time! Go back and reread the first verse in 2 Samuel 11. It ends with the penetrating observation "But David stayed at Jerusalem."

Why didn't he go out to battle like he should have?

Certainly it was customary for the king, the military leader, the commander in chief, to lead his troops as they fought against their enemies. But David didn't. He stayed home.

I can think of several answers why.

Perhaps he was too lazy to go fight. *I am king, and that's tough work,* he could have rationalized. *Especially going off to war—it's so demanding! I think I will delegate this battle to Joab. It will be good experience for him. I'll just get a little R & R. Maybe I'll join them later. After all, I deserve a break today.*

There is a second possibility to consider. David may have hung back from the battle simply because he was a man with too much power and control. Actually, the entire story reads like a power trip to me. He stayed home when he shouldn't have. He was looking at Bathsheba when he shouldn't have. He had her brought to him when he shouldn't have. All were exercises in extreme power. As they say, absolute power corrupts absolutely.

There is a third reason David might have been at the wrong place at the wrong time. Selfishness.

Laziness certainly could have played into his decisions, just as power could have. But the root of all this rebellion was his selfishness—wanting what he wanted when he wanted it. And in that, he illustrates all of us at our worst.

With the background now clear in our minds, we can look at Psalm 51 and understand much better why David experienced such agony deep in his soul. It is a wonderfully authentic psalm, especially powerful in its straightforwardness and vulnerability. But it is important to remember that it is still poetry, and thus it is also rich in its metaphorical language. Let's check out a few of these metaphors that aptly describe the messy situation David—and all of us—have created for ourselves.

WHAT ARE THE METAPHORS FOR OUR MESS?

Here's what Psalm 51:1-3 says:

> *Be gracious to me, O God, according to Your lovingkindness; according to the greatness of your compassion blot out my transgressions. Wash me thoroughly from my iniquity and cleanse me from my sin. For I know my transgressions, and my sin is ever before me.*

The first metaphor that David used comes from the legal world. Put in the language of the lawyer, it translates: *We need our record expunged.* Here's how David said it:

> *Blot out my transgressions.* PSALM 51:1

The Hebrew word for *blot out* is a word that can be translated "wipe out, erase, obliterate, delete." In the courtroom sense, it refers to a clean slate. It means taking the legal record of my crime and wiping it clean, that is, having it *expunged.* (See, I told you this was like a *Law & Order* episode. Can't you just see actor Sam Waterston, in your mind's eye, declaring to the judge that he wants your record expunged? Now that's good television!) In effect, David was requesting a lawyer.

There's a second metaphor developed here as well. *We need our dirty laundry washed.* This word picture appears in the first part of the second verse:

Wash me thoroughly from my iniquity.　PSALM 51:2

Notice David didn't say, "I don't want my dirty laundry *exposed.*" I think that's how most of us react when we see the metaphor of "dirty laundry." *You mean I have to go public so that everyone can see how wicked I am?* No, that's not where David was going with his soiled robes. He said that he wanted them washed. I get the idea that because he was a king, he didn't do his own laundry all that often. So I think he was pleading, not only for a lawyer, but also for a housekeeper.

Here's the third metaphor: *We need our fatal disease cleansed.* Or as David put it:

Cleanse me from my sin.　PSALM 51:2

The most literal way to interpret this verse would be to say, "Cleanse me before it kills me!" The truth is that sin is so deadly, so fatal, so destructive, that we need medical attention to cure us of our condition. In verse 2, David appeared to be asking for a doctor.

The metaphors are rich and varied. To review, we are in need of:

A lawyer for our crime

A housekeeper for our dirty laundry

A doctor for our fatal disease

WHO IS RESPONSIBLE FOR THE MESS?

When I am dealing with big-time guilt, I love to blame the situation on somebody else—maybe it's just the way I handle it. (That's a joke; I know we all think this way.) That's why I find David's words in this psalm so out of the ordinary. Apparently he had already worked through the phase known as blame shifting and was stepping up to the plate to own up to everything himself. Look more carefully at the following verses:

My transgressions (Psalm 51:1, emphasis added)

My iniquity (51:2, emphasis added)

My sin (51:2, emphasis added)

My transgressions (51:3, emphasis added)

My sin (51:3, emphasis added)

Who's responsible? From my point of view, David could have blamed a lot of other people. He could have blamed Bathsheba for not being more discreet in her bathing habits. He could have blamed Uriah for not being attentive to his wife's needs. He could have blamed Nathan, the prophet, who ultimately called him on the entire incident. And certainly he could have blamed God for allowing the whole thing to happen.

But David didn't do any of that. Instead of passing the buck, he said in no uncertain terms for the world to hear: *I am responsible.*

David's admission is an important lesson for us to learn in dealing with our own guilt: Beware of blame shifting. If this incident were a modern-day scenario, I can just imagine the rationalizations and the justifications. But it doesn't work that way. It's not about my upbringing. It's not about my unavailable wife. It's not about my low self-esteem. It's not about my special needs. If fessing up worked for David, it will work for each of us: *I am responsible, so I need to take responsibility.*

David's transparency lets us know who was really responsible for the mess that was created, but there are still lingering questions.

WHERE IS GOD IN RELATION TO MY GUILT?

Once again David made three statements. The first provides the overarching framework for how David viewed God in the midst of his brokenness. *My only hope is in the character of God.*

David addressed the greatness of God right out of the gate:

> *Be gracious to me, O God, according to Your* lovingkindness; *according to the greatness of Your compassion blot out my transgressions.*   PSALM 51:1, *emphasis added*

The word translated "lovingkindness" is one that overflows with meaning in the original. The word in the Hebrew is the word *hesed*, describing the love that comes from God based on His covenant relationship with us. In other words, God is faithful in His love even when we are unfaithful to Him. *Lovingkindness* is another word for *grace*, which so many of us know as undeserved mercy. If God is not a God of love, we are lost. Without the God of compassion, we are lost. David put it this way in another of his psalms:

> *For as high as the heavens are above the earth, so great is His lovingkindness toward those who fear Him.*   PSALM 103:11

There's that word again—*hesed*. It reflects the beauty of God's love. It's unconditional. It says that from God's perspective, even if we do such repulsive things as murder someone after sleeping with his or her spouse, we can still be a part of the family of God. Granted, God is righteous, so He doesn't agree with our sinful decisions, or even condone our disgusting behavior, but He loves us so deeply that He won't hand us our walking papers. With God there are no pink slips. We throw ourselves on His character as the Lord of *hesed* to bring relief from all our guilt and shame.

The second observation David makes concerning God in relation to his guilt is this: *My sin is against Him, above everyone else.*

Here's how David prayed:

Against You, You only, I have sinned and done what is evil in Your sight, so that You are justified when You speak and blameless when You judge.   PSALM 51:4

Once again, no blame shifting. I find it so fascinating that David didn't say he sinned against Uriah, nor did he admit he sinned against Bathsheba. He also didn't confess that he sinned against his wives. His sin was against God. It reminds me of how the Prodigal Son phrased his brokenness when he returned to his father's home:

"Father, I have sinned against heaven *and in your sight; I am no longer worthy to be called your son."*

LUKE 15:21, *emphasis added*

Above all, the son was clear that he had sinned against his Lord. But his father, an earthly version of our heavenly Father, knew exactly what he was going to do when his son returned:

So [the son] got up and came to his father. But while he was still a long way off, his father saw him and felt compassion for him, *and ran and embraced him and kissed him.*

LUKE 15:20, *emphasis added*

Luke was writing in Greek, not Hebrew, but it has the same feel as God's *hesed* to me.

One final statement of how we should relate to

God in all our messiness: *Our attitude should be one of brokenness.*

David writes:

> *The sacrifices of God are a broken spirit; a broken and a contrite heart, O God, You will not despise.*　PSALM 51:17

In today's vernacular, I think David is telling us that it's got to be real. Faking it doesn't cut it with God. When I think of sacrifices in the Old Testament, I think of bringing before God the very best of gifts, like offering the most unblemished lamb. And as important as that was, David is giving us some inside information on what makes sacrifice really happen—the best of gifts don't measure up without the brokenness that needs to accompany them.

David knew the utterly depleted nature of brokenness. In an earlier psalm he wrote:

> *The righteous cry, and the LORD hears and delivers them out of all their troubles. The LORD is near to the brokenhearted and saves those who are crushed in spirit.*　PSALM 34:17-18

Those of us who have felt broken beyond repair can take great comfort in the fact that God is near to us in our brokenness and that He will heal our crushed spirits.

HOW DO I GET RID OF THE GUILT?

> *I acknowledged my sin to You, and my iniquity I did not hide; I said, "I will* confess *my transgressions to the LORD"; and You* forgave *the guilt of my sin.*　PSALM 32:5, *emphasis added*

From the time I was a little kid, I understood the principle of forgiveness and how it worked. When I sin, I acknowledge my sin by confessing it to God, and He, in turn, offers me forgiveness. But notice how David frames the process of ridding himself of his guilt and his shame. He returns to one of his favorite forms (and mine too)—the use of metaphors. First he says:

Purify me with hyssop, and I shall be clean.   PSALM 51:7

Most of us don't deal much with hyssop, so let me provide you with some inside information. Hyssop is a plant. In Bible times, it wasn't just another pretty plant—it had a more significant function. It was actually used to clean lepers in hopes that it would cure them, and it was also used in the preparation of dead bodies for burial. Think of it as an Old Testament version of being sterilized.

David then says: *Wash me.*

Wash me, and I shall be whiter than snow.   PSALM 51:7

I love this word picture because I know what freshly fallen snow is like. Growing up in Philadelphia, I know all about city snow. It is pure and white for only a short time before it turns into dirty, slushy, salty, ugly snow. But God is not talking about Philly snow. He is talking about the real, pure deal. That is important for us to cling to, for God is not given to halfway solutions. He will not bring us pure snow, only to have it messed up by the dirt of the city. No, God will forgive us, and in doing so He will cleanse us completely.

David's next poetic phrase is: *Restore my joy.*

Make me to hear joy and gladness. . . . Restore to me the joy of Your salvation.   PSALM 51:8, 12

God wants us to have joy in our lives. He is as displeased as we are when our behavior has gotten us into another pickle. By acknowledging our wrongdoing through confession, we can experience God's forgiveness, which is the path back to joy. We don't have to live under a dark cloud of guilt. We don't need to be developing stomach ulcers because of our personal shame. Christ came to forgive us, and our responsibility is to live as holy as we can. But when we blow it, we need to tap into His forgiveness and move ahead in our lives.

Fourth and finally, David asks God to: *Forgive my sins.*

Hide Your face from my sins, and blot out all my iniquities.
PSALM 51:9

We come to confess as broken people, and we forsake the sin that we have done. David wrote of this very same thing in another psalm:

I acknowledged my sin to You, and my iniquity I did not hide; I said, "I will confess *my transgressions to the LORD;" and You* forgave the guilt of my sin.   PSALM 32:5, *emphasis added*

Wow, did you see those words I highlighted? If we acknowledge our sin to God by confessing it, the Lord will forgive not only our sin but the guilt of our sin.

Bingo. It is an Old Testament 1 John 1:9.

If we confess our sins, He is faithful and righteous to forgive us our sins and to cleanse us from all unrighteousness.

WHAT IS A PRACTICAL PLAN FOR AVOIDING GUILT?

Just because we have the forgiveness of our heavenly Father does not mean we should pursue a lifestyle of wrongdoing. "Oh, I can do whatever I want and then just confess it to God and He'll forgive me—it's a great plan." No, that's not what God had in mind when He designed us. He wants us to take the high road, the right road, the holy one. Let's look at some practical steps to avoid guilt altogether.

First, if you're thinking about straying—forget it! You can rise above the evil thoughts that tell you to steal the baseball cards, or lie to your boss, or sleep with a woman and then murder her husband. Not only does God forgive you in order to release you from your guilt, but He also gives you the power of the Holy Spirit to be victorious over your sinful thoughts and desires in the first place. Power over sin is life at its best. If you can live in God's power, you can avoid guilt entirely. Imagine how good that would feel!

Second, if you're beyond thinking about fooling around and find yourself already sinning—flee! That's the word the apostle Paul used when writing Timothy:

Flee from youthful lusts.   2 TIMOTHY 2:22

Flee means stop it. Give it up. Get as far away from it as you possibly can. Is someone seducing you? Run from him or her—as fast as you can. Are you lured by Internet pornography? Stay clear of those sites as best you can with the help of software locks and filters and whatever else you can find to eliminate easy access. Are you already involved in an immoral situation? Get out of it. Run from it. End it. Walk away. It is such a simple strategy, yet anyone who is entangled in sin will tell you it is extremely difficult to do. But with God's power, you can be victorious.

Finally, what if you are someone who has fooled around in the past? Forgiveness is available to you. That is what this chapter has been all about. I'm not condoning what you have done. But I'm offering you the plan that God put in place for every one of us in order to relieve us from the guilt and shame that weigh us down.

Forgiveness is how you are able to move past the pain and get on with your life. When you are forgiven by God, you are freed, you are released. When you forgive somebody else, you release that person.

When my marriage dissolved all those years ago, there were five children caught in the cross fire. Each of our kids has processed the divorce differently, but all have experienced their share of pain.

My son Joseph had to deal with the divorce differently from his siblings simply because he was the youngest. In many ways, I felt the greatest distance between myself and Joseph, even though he never really showed any ill will toward me in the painful aftermath.

The defining moment for me came many years later. I was speaking at the weekend services for a church just outside of Las Vegas in Henderson, Nevada. My oldest son, Jesse, and Joseph had accompanied my wife, Kathi, and me because my sons were doing special music for the weekend. I love these weekends when we all work together. To be able to speak right before or right after my sons have sung is a feeling beyond description.

This particular church has a Saturday evening service as well as three Sunday morning services. After the Saturday night service, the four of us were sitting around a table at one of our favorite restaurants in Henderson, reflecting on the evening's activities and beyond.

It was the beyond that rocked my world. Somehow Jesse and Joseph began talking about how they dealt with the divorce. Some things both boys said were familiar to me because I had heard them before. But in the midst of the familiar came this jolt from my youngest:

"You know, Dad, there was a time there where I really hated you."

I was stunned. *Hated me?* I thought to myself. "I thought everything was cool between the two of us."

"Yeah, I had a lot of anger built up inside. I hated my life, and I blamed you."

The silence was deafening.

"But then I just decided to release you."

Release you. In those two powerful words, my son was describing how he put forgiveness into action. I have never forgotten that evening's conversation, and I don't think I ever will.

Several weeks later, Joseph sent me an e-mail with a set of lyrics he and Jesse had been working on for a song he wanted to include on his new CD. The song is "I Release You." Joseph has given me permission to include the lyrics here. I hope that you will read them slowly in order to grasp their fullest meaning and their power. The lyrics emphasize releasing someone who needs to be forgiven. Do you have someone like that in your life?

I Release You

Rolling towards the future,
Tangled in the past,
Bitter roots are planted
And they're holding me back.

Climbing towards contentment,
With chains around my neck,

Heading for the sky,
But sinking down instead.

And if the wind should catch me,
The anchor's still attached.
And I can see I'm drowning slowly,
But still I can't let go, 'til I release you.

My shadow stood before me
But now it casts behind,
Yesterday has fallen
But today is in the light.

Battle scars remind me
Of fighting in the war,
I won't forget the battle,
But won't settle the score.

I can begin drifting forward
'Til the next time I falter,
I can still remember,
But proclaim I'm bigger.
I release you.
I release me.
I release you.

FOUR

CHAPTER

THE LESSON FROM THE ORANGE BOWL

ANYONE WHO HAS ever heard me speak knows that when I get my arms around a good story, I never let it go. Part of what makes a good story a good story is that it has the versatility to illustrate dozens of different concepts.

Such is the case with one of my favorite stories of all time. It is a true story that took place in Miami in late 1972. I know the following fact will leave many of my readers in a state of stunned disbelief, but it is, nonetheless, the honest truth . . .

I was a member of the 1972 Miami Dolphins football organization.

What makes that statement even more incredible to any football fan is that 1972 was the only year in NFL history that a team had gone undefeated. We were 17–0 and defeated the Washington Redskins in the Super Bowl in early 1973. Don Shula was at the helm as head coach. In those days I was known for my side-to-side agility as well as a rocket throwing arm. Hard to believe? Perhaps I should, ahem, clarify . . .

1972 was the year I sold programs during the NFL games at the Orange Bowl.

Now before you scoff, cluck your tongue, and roll your eyes, I want you to know that the program salesmen are as much a part of the team as the uniformed men on the field during the game. To begin with, we all arrive at the stadium around the same time. Somewhere between 8 and 9 a.m., just as the first team bus is arriving at the stadium, the program salesmen begin manning their positions on the outside and the inside perimeters of the stadium. Three minutes after arriving, we were met by a man driving a forklift. He was carrying our pallets filled with programs. He kindly, yet unceremoniously, dumped each of our pallets right next to us. Now we were ready to begin selling programs. There was only one glitch. . . .

There were no fans at the stadium that early.

Not to be discouraged, the loyal band of program salesmen met in a prescribed section of the Orange Bowl to observe the warm-up activities down on the field. We gathered at the highest elevation in the Orange Bowl, "the nosebleed section," to avoid being a nuisance to the players below.

We carried out this routine every week we had a home game. Most mornings we would watch the teams come out on the field in just shorts and T-shirts—no pads or helmets—to warm up, greet old friends on the opposing team, and just get into the groove for the game.

But there is one game I will never forget. It was the last home game of the season, and that meant one highly anticipated event: the Punt, Pass, and Kick competition. For years the Ford Motor Company sponsored this event, featuring kids from ages six to twelve competing in those three football skills to win some valuable prizes. On this day, the merry band of program salesmen (myself included) were watching the dress rehearsal of the halftime show, which would feature the contest. The finalists looked impressive, assembled on the field in exact-replica Miami Dolphins uniforms. The littlest guy was the cutest, of course. He looked like a helmet with a pair of cleats sticking out from the bottom of the jersey.

Each of these youngsters would have one opportunity to throw a pass on the field of the Orange Bowl, on live television, for all the world to see. (Can you believe there really was a time when the television networks didn't break away for a halftime recap show but actually *showed* the entire halftime festivities? Think of it as P.E.—Pre ESPN.)

As we watched, a man on the field walked the kids through the routine. He had to be the director, for he was, in fact, directing. He navigated each child, one at a time, to the forty-yard line, made a motion with his arm as if he were passing a football, and then gestured to the sideline on his left where each contestant needed to stand when his or her turn was over.

After all the participants had been walked through this exercise and it appeared everyone understood what to do, the man began to lead the kids off the field single file to wait in the clubhouse.

But wait . . . the youngest player decided to make a bold move. He purposely lagged behind the others, successfully breaking away from the line.

He was alone, on the turf of the Orange Bowl, in a miniature version of an official Miami Dolphins uniform.

Talk about fantasy football! Our contingent of program salesmen couldn't take our eyes off him.

Not wasting a moment of time, he called his imaginary team together in an imaginary huddle. He was the quarterback, strolling confidently up to the line of scrimmage.

He positioned himself behind the imaginary center, ready to receive the snap. He was barking signals, looking to his left, then looking to his right, making certain all his offensive line knew he was calling an audible. He took the snap and quickly fell back into the imaginary pocket, trusting his line to block for him while he looked for an open receiver.

This was where his imaginary game began to get into trouble. Our little guy started scrambling. Up in the bleachers, the program salesmen were doing their best to remain quiet.

Wait! He finally saw a man open, and he heaved the pretend football as far as he could throw. It was a bomb of a pass, a Hail Mary, the whole enchilada, for certain. How could we be so sure? Because the pass was so long, our little guy had enough time to be magically transformed from a Miami Dolphins quarterback to a Miami Dolphins wide receiver!

Now he was running down the sideline at full sprint. Without warning, he cut to the inside, the classic post pattern. Leaping into the air, our hero brought down the imaginary pass and looked ahead to the fifty-plus yards that separated him from the goal line.

We mistakenly concluded he would run straight to the end zone. Wrong. He had multiple defenders to defeat. So once again, our little helmet with cleats began running from one side of the football field to the other, sidestepping players, doing his best impersonation of the Heisman Trophy statue, and a host of other amazing moves. I could only imagine what he was imagining!

Up in the stands we could barely contain our enthusiasm. We wanted to cheer wildly, but we knew that if he knew we were watching him, it would be game over. So biting our lips to keep from yelling, we watched this wonderful display of unleashed youthful imagination.

He had turned a run of no more than fifty yards into a run of just over a couple of miles. With all the zigging and zagging, he barely had the stamina to make it all the way. It was already hot under the blazing Miami sun, and the extra weight and thickness of the uniform were not helping. Yes, he was officially sweating buckets. But eventually he made it to the goal line. Upon entering the end zone, he performed a string of wild dance moves. Remember, it was 1972 and the taunting penalty was not yet in effect. (For those of you who can remember back that far, he had a particularly polished version of the end-zone dance made popular by Billy "White Shoes" Johnson!)

Once he scored, the program salesmen could no longer hold back our cheering. We'd been well-behaved long enough. We all rose to our feet, waving our hands, stomping our feet, and cheering wildly for the best football show we had seen all season. We loved this kid and wanted to thank him.

But, just as we had figured, once he knew he was being watched, he felt embarrassed. When he spotted us, we could see the life being sucked out of him. He seemed to roll off the field as quickly as was humanly possible to avoid any further personal humiliation.

The program salesmen continued to have a good laugh

over what we had just observed. In the midst of all that good-natured kidding, I came up with a suggestion. "Isn't it a shame we couldn't have worked it out for that little kid to actually run a play against the real Miami Dolphins defense? What a thrill that would have been for the little guy!"

My comrades looked at me in disbelief. "You've got to be kidding, right? The No Name defense of the Dolphins would destroy that kid."

Looking back, they were probably right, but I still think it would have been cool to see him go up against them. I just wanted the little guy to really fulfill a six-year-old's fantasy.

I guess it is one thing to have an imaginary obstacle to overcome and quite another thing to have an obstacle that is real. But this story illustrates an even more difficult circumstance—multiple obstacles. That poor little kid would have faced not one, but many men on the opposing defensive line. So my friends were right, it wasn't a kind thing to wish for him.

I have never forgotten the image of that little guy running down the field, overcoming multiple adversaries, even though they were figments of his imagination. He ran with such grace, such dignity, such determination. There's something about the way that kid handled that situation that inspires me when my life resembles a field full of NFL defense players the size of large mountains, going up against me—the helmet with the set of cleats.

I want the same kind of victory that little child experienced. I want to feel as if no matter how big the obstacle is, no matter how many there are or how overwhelming they may appear, I can overcome each and every one of them.

Some of you who are reading these pages have seen strategies to overcome individual obstacles in your life, but you have had this nagging thought in the back of your mind: *I wish I had only one adversary to overcome, but I've got multiple obstacles in my life!* Maybe it's not just your boss but a series of coworkers as well. It's not just a rebellious teen, it's a spouse who doesn't realize the significance of these behaviors. It's not just the cancer, but the treatments that incapacitate you on top of the disease. Team them up however you will, it all comes down to overwhelming adversity. It's fancy talk for what most folks think of as "piling on."

Are you facing more than one adversary in your life right now? God knows what that looks like, and He gives us a historical account that offers a glimpse of how we can be victorious. It is tucked away in a not-very-often-read section of the Old Testament. But I promise that when we're through reading it, you will be exclaiming, "Jumpin' Jehoshaphat!"

4

MILE MARKER

VICTORY OVER OVERWHELMING ADVERSITY

I'M SURE GLAD this book didn't end a couple of chapters ago. All my life I have run into people who have had their share of overwhelming adversity. But the older I get, the more I run into folks who are dealing with multiple issues all at the same time. "I need this book because I'm currently dealing with issues you mentioned in an earlier chapter as well as issues in later chapters," they may be saying. But isn't there a chapter for men and women who are in that predicament? A single chapter addressing the issue of facing more than one adversity?

Yes, that is what this chapter is all about. And as has

been the case throughout the book, the strategies discussed here are based on the principles of Scripture.

Buried deep in the Old Testament is the story of someone facing multiple obstacles. It's a rather lengthy portion of the Bible, but I would like you to read it slowly and carefully in its entirety before we break it down. It's military history, a sort of ancient, nonfiction W. E. B. Griffin. Observe how this magnificent story unfolds:

After this, the armies of the Moabites, Ammonites, and some of the Meunites declared war on Jehoshaphat. Messengers came and told Jehoshaphat, "A vast army from Edom is marching against you from beyond the Dead Sea. They are already at Hazazon-tamar." (This was another name for En-gedi.)

Jehoshaphat was terrified by this news and begged the LORD for guidance. He also ordered everyone in Judah to begin fasting. So people from all the towns of Judah came to Jerusalem to seek the LORD's help.

Jehoshaphat stood before the community of Judah and Jerusalem in front of the new courtyard at the Temple of the LORD. He prayed, "O LORD, God of our ancestors, you alone are the God who is in heaven. You are ruler of all the kingdoms of the earth. You are powerful and mighty; no one can stand against you! O our God, did you not drive out those who lived in this land when your people Israel arrived? And did you not give this land forever to the descendants of your friend Abraham? Your people settled here and built this Temple to honor your name. They said, 'Whenever we are faced with any calamity such as war, plague, or famine, we can come to stand in your presence before this Temple where your name is honored. We can cry out to you to save us, and you will hear us and rescue us.'

"And now see what the armies of Ammon, Moab, and Mount Seir are doing. You would not let our ancestors invade those nations when Israel left Egypt, so they went around them and did not destroy them. Now see how they reward us! For they have come to throw us out of your land, which you gave us as an inheritance. O our God, won't you stop them? We are powerless against this mighty army that is about to attack us. We do not know what to do, but we are looking to you for help."

As all the men of Judah stood before the LORD with their little ones, wives, and children, the Spirit of the LORD came upon one of the men standing there. His name was Jahaziel son of Zechariah, son of Benaiah, son of Jeiel, son of Mattaniah, a Levite who was a descendant of Asaph.

He said, "Listen, all you people of Judah and Jerusalem! Listen, King Jehoshaphat! This is what the LORD says: Do not be afraid! Don't be discouraged by this mighty army, for the battle is not yours, but God's. Tomorrow, march out against them. You will find them coming up through the ascent of Ziz at the end of the valley that opens into the wilderness of Jeruel. But you will not even need to fight. Take your positions; then stand still and watch the LORD's victory. He is with you, O people of Judah and Jerusalem. Do not be afraid or discouraged. Go out against them tomorrow, for the LORD *is with you!"*

Then King Jehoshaphat bowed low with his face to the ground. And all the people of Judah and Jerusalem did the same, worshiping the LORD. *Then the Levites from the clans of Kohath and Korah stood to praise the* LORD, *the God of Israel, with a very loud shout.*

Early the next morning the army of Judah went out into the wilderness of Tekoa. On the way Jehoshaphat stopped and said, "Listen to me, all you people of Judah and Jerusalem! Believe in the LORD *your God, and you will be able to stand firm. Believe in his prophets, and you will succeed."*

After consulting the people, the king appointed singers to walk ahead of the army, singing to the LORD *and praising him for his holy splendor. This is what they sang: "Give thanks to the* LORD; *his faithful love endures forever!"*

At the very moment they began to sing and give praise, the LORD *caused the armies of Ammon, Moab, and Mount Seir to start fighting among themselves. The armies of Moab and Ammon turned against their allies from Mount Seir and killed every one of them. After they had destroyed the army of Seir, they began attacking each other. So when the army of Judah arrived at the lookout point in the wilderness, all they saw were dead bodies lying on the ground as far as they could see. Not a single one of the enemy had escaped.*

King Jehoshaphat and his men went out to gather the plunder. They found vast amounts of equipment, clothing, and other valuables—more than they could carry. There was so much plunder that it took them three days just to collect it all! On the fourth day they gathered in the Valley of Blessing, which got its name that day because the people praised and thanked the LORD there. It is still called the Valley of Blessing today.

Then all the men returned to Jerusalem, with Jehoshaphat leading them, overjoyed that the LORD had given them victory over their enemies. They marched into Jerusalem to the music of harps, lyres, and trumpets, and they proceeded to the Temple of the LORD.

When all the surrounding kingdoms heard that the LORD himself had fought against the enemies of Israel, the fear of God came over them. So Jehoshaphat's kingdom was at peace, for his God had given him rest on every side.

2 CHRONICLES 20:1-30, NLT

I warned you it was a long passage—but it was worth the effort, wasn't it? God delivered Jehoshaphat and his kingdom from multiple adversaries.

Let's break the story into four parts: the Setup, the Strategy, the Battle, and the Blessing. We can learn important truths from all four aspects.

THE SETUP

This dramatic historical account begins with the following important words:

A vast army *from Edom is marching against you from beyond the Dead Sea.*   v. 2, *emphasis added*

"There is an enemy out there," God told Jehoshaphat—or more precisely, "There are enemies, plural, out there." That's our first observation.

Maybe you know what that feels like. "It felt like things were just piling on," my new friend Matthew (not his real name) told me over coffee one morning. "My life just felt like it was coming apart at the seams. Every time I thought it couldn't get worse, it did! I felt completely overwhelmed."

"Tell me how it unfolded," I encouraged.

"Well, it all started when I got sick," he recalled. "Here I am, fifty years old, and the doctor tells me I have this condition that is a major concern. He tells me it's not going to kill me, but it will seriously compromise my quality of life."

"And did it?" I asked.

"Yes," he answered emphatically. "Not so much at first. The main issue was fatigue. It felt like each passing day brought with it a greater sense of being worn out. I was so tired that it began to take its toll. First I gave it all at the office, which meant I came home exhausted. My wife was hoping for a little help around the house, a little bit of interest in her world, but I was just too slammed to offer it to her."

"That's a tough one," I lamented.

"Oh, that's only the beginning," Matthew said with a large, dramatic sigh. "The more the fatigue ate away at my energy, the less effective I was at work."

"Uh-oh," I muttered, fearing where this was going.

"Yup. The boss was as helpful as he could be, but ultimately he couldn't look away any longer. I was not fulfilling my job responsibilities, so I was let go."

"So you've got a medical condition and you've just lost your job," I summarized. "That qualifies as overwhelming adversity."

"You're right, but that's not where it ended."

"Okay, finish the story," I invited, hoping for the proverbial happy ending.

"It got worse," he began, and my heart sunk.

"You would think this whole catastrophe could have provided an excellent opportunity for my wife and me to grow closer together. But it didn't. It was just the opposite. It was as if the added pressure in my life caused my mate to buckle. Without any forewarning, my wife announced she was moving out about a month after the job went away. I was crushed. How could she leave me at such a painful time? I needed her more than ever. But she had found a convenient diversion in the form of another man— a healthy man. And as they say, the rest is history."

Matthew understood multiple adversaries in his life. Sick, no job, broken relationship—the poor guy had just explained to me the trifecta of pain.

The rest of Matthew's story parallels the story we're reading in Second Chronicles. Notice the second observation: Adversity causes us to worry and experience fear.

It is stated simply in the text:

Jehoshaphat was terrified . . . v. 3, *emphasis added*

Just like Jehoshaphat, Matthew was filled with panic. "How could all of this be happening to me?" he cried out to the Lord. "This is the kind of stuff that should happen to sinful, heathen people—not guys like me! I'm a good person. I try to serve God as best I can. This is so unfair!"

All of us have heard these words. Many of us have uttered them ourselves. But look back at the story of Jehoshaphat. This brings us to our third observation: Adversity, worry, and fear can cause us to draw closer to the Lord.

Jehoshaphat was afraid. But what did he do with that fear?

. . . and begged the LORD for guidance. v. 3

He used that fear to focus more intently on his Lord. Pain usually sends us to the extremes. We're either pulled further away from God or drawn closer to Him. In this passage, our hero moves in the right direction.

That's good advice for you, too, my friend. After all, drawing closer to God worked in a very positive way for our buddy Jehoshaphat.

Let's examine the strategy God passed on to Jehoshaphat, instructions that if followed would result in victory over his multiple adversaries.

THE STRATEGY

God began by having Jehoshaphat state the most basic premise in our understanding of victory: Power over adversity is in God's hands. No one can touch Him!

As it says in the text:

You are powerful and mighty; no one can stand against you! v. 6

If we're going to be victorious against our multiple enemies, it is not going to be because of any human strategy or advantage. It is all coming from the Lord.

Again, that doesn't mean we are off the hook and out of the picture. No, it's just the opposite. God wants us to exercise our faith and trust Him.

Notice the second part of the strategy: We give it all to God. He will hear us and take care of us.

I love the way it reads in the text:

We can come to stand in your presence. . . . We can cry out to you *to save us, and you will hear us and rescue us.*

v. 9, *emphasis added*

We *cry* to Him. Some of us can relate to that word in a big way. Life is so painful, so traumatic, so dysfunctional that all we can do is fall on our face and scream out to God, "Please do something to help me!"

And the beauty is that He hears our cries. In the text, the people of Judah weren't flat on their faces in despair; they were still able to stand. But I just love the rapid-fire succession of verbs in that verse: we stand, we cry, You hear, You rescue.

The next part of the plan should sound familiar to you: Our adversity is overwhelming. We are powerless and without answers. Our eyes are on God.

Feel the great emotion in this verse:

We are powerless against this mighty army that is about to attack us. We do not know what to do, but we are looking to you for help. v. 12

We are *powerless* against our enemies. It sounds like the beginning of a 12-step support group, doesn't it? The reason groups like that are so effective is that they have capitalized on this key point: We can't do it on our own. We surrender our will to the One who can do it—God Himself.

Notice also that we are once again encouraged to place our eyes on the Lord. Remember Peter frantically trying to walk on the water? It was a successful venture as long as he focused on Jesus. Focus requires more than vision; it requires an unwavering fix on our God.

"Use this strategy, and you will be victorious," God

says in so many words. Let's see how the strategy played out in Jehoshaphat's battle.

THE BATTLE

First, notice the battle is the Lord's. The text records it this way:

> *The battle is not yours, but God's.*   v. 15

Sound familiar? If you know your Bible, it should. Those same words are words that encouraged Gideon in his battle. Those same words are words that encouraged David in his epic one-on-one battle with the giant, Goliath.

In other words, to rewrite a phrase that you often hear: It's *not* all about us. The chorus to this song is being sung over and over again. There will be victory, but it's not because we are amazing. It's because God is.

There is a second principle here that is one of the most important in the entire account: We don't need to fight, but we do need to stand in order to see God deliver us.

> *You will not even need to fight. Take your positions; then stand still and watch the LORD's victory.*   v. 17

By now, you may have guessed that I'm a big football fan. I am always thrilled when I receive an invitation to speak to a professional sports team, especially an NFL team. The more I do it, the more I realize each one is just that—a team. Most of us get so excited about the prospect of hanging out with the quarterback or the running back or the wide receiver—the marquee players—that we forget about the other eight guys who make their glory possible—the offensive linemen!

These guys are some of God's greatest creations—both in girth and heart. They love life and realize they have a job to do to make their team successful. So whenever I am with them, I love to ask them the most basic of questions, to glean insight from guys who make their living working in the trenches.

On one occasion, I was surrounded by an especially talkative group of linemen, so I fired away. "Hey guys, I have a question for you. Since I have never played football on a team with a coach, I am wondering why he requires you to get down into that awkward-looking three-point or four-point stance. Why can't you just break from the huddle, walk up to the line of scrimmage, and stand there? Is that bending and setting up all that necessary?"

They looked at one another, rolled their eyes in wonder and disbelief, and turned to look at me. One lineman cleared his throat and said, "Our line coach has put it into four little words: 'Prepare to get hit!'"

Now, I'm not an athlete (I think I've made that point clearly), but I like using athletic terms as metaphors for life. I may get a defender pushing right up against me. I may get two or three defenders trying to run right over me. I may find that once the ball is hiked I have no one across from me, because my opponents are ganging up on a teammate of mine. What happens isn't the point. The point is that *I am prepared* for something to happen.

I believe this is what God had in mind when He sent the army of Judah out to battle that day. Being God, He knew, of course, that He would defeat the enemies with a more creative strategy. Consequently, He could have instructed the army to take the day off. "Go swim in the river, or spend a day back home with your family!" But no, God required that the army come out in full preparation for battle and *stand*.

Why would the Lord require such a posture? He requires it in order to show us that we cannot even consider assuming a position of passivity. We need to prepare to get hit. Sure, God will win the battle for us—the battle is the Lord's—but He still wants us to show up.

The concept of "taking your stand" is one that appears often in the Old Testament. And it always seems to zero in on the same idea: God will deliver us, but we still have to make the effort by at least showing up. The Lord instructed Moses to tell the children of Israel the same thing right before the miraculous parting of the Red Sea. It worked back then, and it will work for you today.

The third principle for battle is this: Even in the middle of our adversity, we must still keep our focus on the Lord.

It's quite a dramatic moment in the story:

Then King Jehoshaphat bowed low with his face to the ground . . . worshiping the LORD. v. 18

Once again, it comes down to faith. Can you trust God to deliver you? It really doesn't look that difficult until you start to fill in the details. Perhaps your life is like my friend Matthew's, a man dealing with so much adversity. Is it easy to trust God when deep down inside you are still bewildered as to why He allowed the sickness to occur in the first place? Is it easy to trust God when you give 110 percent at the office, but because of your health, it still isn't enough? Is it easy to trust God when the love of your life walks away?

No, it's not easy, but it is still required. It's not simple, but it's right. It is never wrong to put your trust in God. Even though it may look bleak right now, remember: God will never disappoint you.

A case in point is Jehoshaphat.

THE BLESSING

Three statements leading up to the climax of this story send chills up my spine every time I read them. They all add up to big-time encouragement. Here's the first one: *Our adversaries will stand against each other and destroy each other.*

Look what happened to all of Jehoshaphat's enemies!

The armies of Moab and Ammon turned against their allies from Mount Seir and killed every one of them. After they had destroyed the army of Seir, they began attacking each other. v. 23

Jehoshaphat's army did what was required of them, showing up for the battle, only to discover that their enemies had been fighting against each other. And ultimately, they destroyed each other! If you are reading these words as you are facing more than one adversary, you are probably smiling with glee at the thought of something like that happening in your particular circumstance.

Your obstacles might be more complicated than the battle in Second Chronicles, but God can handle them. For so many of us, the name of the game these days is *wait*.

We're being faithful. We're trusting God. But nothing seems to be happening. Hang in there, friend. Just because it isn't happening now doesn't mean it isn't going to happen. It's all a matter of timing—God's perfect timing.

Matthew is growing impatient. Upon reading the story of Jehoshaphat, my friend conjured up a scenario in his mind: He was going to be miraculously healed and his boss was going to rehire him (after being laid up from an accident involving a drunk driver who just happened to be Matthew's wife's new boyfriend). No more sickness, job back intact, boyfriend serving hard time for DUI!

You have to give Matthew credit for creativity. But the truth is none of that has happened. Things are still pretty upside down. Matthew's faith is being tested by the Lord through this character-building time of waiting.

But trust me, God will deliver. We don't know when, and we don't know how. But He will.

And when He does, we will see the second blessing: *We will reap the rewards for a long time.*

God has a reason for these trials and tribulations. Some of it has to do with the extent of the reward:

> *There was so much plunder that it took them three days just to collect it all!*   v. 25

Did you catch that phrase? It took them three days to gather up all the bounty from the fallen enemies. Why did it take so long? Don't you remember? Because there were multiple enemies. Most likely, they could take the spoils of one enemy in a day. But because there were so many enemies, it was a seventy-two-hour process.

Can you even imagine that outcome in your situation? Because of all you have been asked to endure, your reward is so extensive that it may take you the rest of your life to fully appreciate it! Are you up for that kind of life?

There is a wonderful finale to this great story: *We will have joy, peace, and rest on every side.*

The men returned . . . overjoyed that the LORD had given them victory over their enemies. . . . So Jehoshaphat's kingdom was at peace, for God had given him rest on every side.

vv. 27, 30

I love the sound of that phrase "rest on every side." Our overwhelming obstacles are gone. It's a time of peace and a time of rest. It's not the scenario of "as soon as I get out of one jam, I fall into another one." No, it's quiet. It's reflective. It's peaceful.

It is our reward for being faithful to a God who promises to be faithful to us.

Overwhelming obstacles? No problem. With God in our lives, we can overcome anything.

It happened to me. Granted, it took some time for me to heal from my divorce. There were therapists to see, friendships to build, lessons to learn, and patience to develop.

But after seven years, I felt whole again. Not too long after that, I met Kathi, who became my wife. My kids did their best to be understanding and patient with me, and as a result, our relationship today is strong. My career has returned as well—this time with additional dimensions and greater depth.

Yes, God used His time wisely with me, and consequently I am on my way down the mountain.

In fact, it's in my rearview mirror.

AFTERWORD

THE LESSON FROM VINKO BOGATAJ

ARE YOU OLD enough to remember the classic ABC television show *Wide World of Sports*? Each week the network would go "spanning the globe" to find a veritable cornucopia of athletic endeavors from every continent. Ice-skating, soccer, Greco-Roman wrestling, ping-pong, gymnastics, and curling . . . you name it! My personal favorite was the annual appearance of basketball's great Harlem Globetrotters. I still think Meadowlark Lemon is one of the most hilarious guys I have ever seen.

Beyond the sports coverage itself, *Wide World of Sports* had a most memorable aspect to it. Week after week, during the opening montage, host Jim McKay would introduce the program, including its most famous phrase: "the thrill of victory and the agony of defeat."

If you are like me, you can't remember the video clip used to illustrate *the thrill of victory*. Actually, I think that's because they were constantly changing that image.

But we all remember the agony of defeat. A seemingly sad, hapless ski jumper is shown losing his balance on his way down a ski ramp, tumbling over and over, skis and poles flying wildly in every direction. His image is permanently branded into *WWS* viewers' brains.

What most of us forget, however, is that this individual is a real person.

His name is Vinko Bogataj.

Vinko was competing for his home country of Yugoslavia at the World Ski Flying Championships in Oberstdorf, West Germany, on March 21, 1970. It had been snowing all day. By the time Vinko came up for his third jump, the new snow had made the jump slicker and faster than he was used to. When Vinko attempted to slow himself down, he lost his balance, and the rest we have seen over and over, including his crash through a retaining fence into the crowd of spectators. Even though the crash was rather spectacular, Vinko suffered only a mild concussion.

But Vinko never regained the form that had made him a competitive ski jumper. His highest finish was fifty-seventh place. He eventually dropped out of competitive ski jumping and became a teacher and coach. Yet Vinko found success in other areas. He successfully coached the 1991 world champion Slovenian ski jumper. He married, and today the Bogataj family, which includes two daughters, is living a quiet life in Slovenia.

Well, almost quiet. Due to his cultural-icon status, Vinko was invited to a party thrown by ABC Sports in celebration of the thirty-year anniversary of *Wide World of Sports*. He was blown away by how many people wanted his autograph—even Muhammad Ali.

All because of that tumble.

All because of the agony of defeat.

This book has been written in order to help you avoid becoming a human symbol of defeat like Vinko. I want you to know that you can join me in a new group I am forming. I call it the Not Like Vinko Association, or NLVA for short. There is no charge to belong to NLVA, no registration required. Actually, there are no meetings or scheduled events on the calendar either. There are no officers or board of directors. It's just folks like you and me, bonded together by our battles.

NLVA exists to help folks understand that they can rise above their shortcomings and reign victorious through God's strength. We all fall short, take our tumbles, and crash wildly into the crowd. But God promises to lift us up from our deepest heartache and despair, offering us a better road ahead.

The apostle Peter said it best:

Therefore, humble yourselves under the mighty hand of God, that He may exalt you at the proper time, casting all your anxiety on Him, because He cares for you.   1 PETER 5:6-7

Do you feel humbled? Pain, struggles, and the battles of life can do that to you, can't they? But adversity turns out to be good news. For it is in our humility that God exalts us. In other words, it is only through our battles that we can experience victory. It makes sense, doesn't it?

God exalts us "at the proper time." That is always a big issue for me. I am learning to trust God's calendar more and more as I grow older. Granted, His victory and His deliverance are still not quick enough for my humanity, but I am learning patience in the process.

And I am learning the last part of that passage as well. There is absolutely no value in me keeping my anxiety to myself. No, I need to give it to God. He can handle it. He knows ways of dealing with it that I have never even considered.

I turn it over to Him because He cares for me. Think about that. Why would God love me so? I don't know, but I am so grateful that He does!

Okay, so there really isn't a Not Like Vinko Association, but I hope you see my point. We all have our issues, we all have our struggles, that is very clear. The struggles will continue until we get to heaven. But before that happens, we want to be people known more for our victories than for our defeats.

You and I have a tendency to be Vinkos. Doubt, fear, guilt, or despair grips us to the point that we find it difficult to function in a normal, healthy manner. But through these pages, I hope you have discovered some practical strategies to gain victories in our ongoing battles.

Yes, there are mountains ahead, what seem to be overwhelming obstacles. But God has overcome them, and He will help us do the same through His strength. This is God's truth, the whole truth and nothing but.

Every day you're faced with choices that will impact your future.

What choice will you make today?

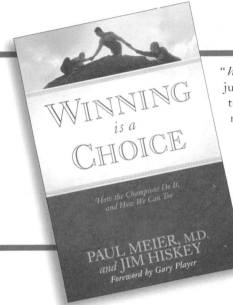

" *Winning is a Choice* is not just for the athlete. It's for the teenager, housewife, teacher, mentor, businessman, or stateswoman. Give this book to someone you love or someone facing adversity and it may well become one of the greatest books they'll ever possess."

Gary Player, pro golfer

Through the inspiring stories of real-life champions, including famous figures such as Tiger Woods and Lance Armstrong as well as everyday people, golf pro Jim Hiskey and well-known psychiatrist Paul Meier outline the eight critical choices that champions face, and demonstrate that the real winners are individuals who make wise decisions when confronted with adversity.

"IF COMPETITION WERE A VIRUS, WE WOULD HAVE AN EPIDEMIC ON OUR HANDS."

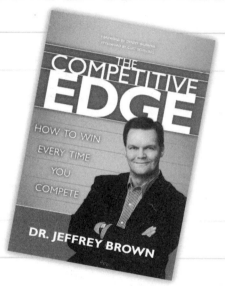

We all face competition every day, and we all want to win. But can you still be a serious competitor if you value qualities like character and integrity? Even better, can these attributes actually *help* you on your way to the top?

Clinical and sport psychologist Dr. Jeffrey Brown says that the answer is yes. Identifying seven crucial principles that will guide you to victory every time you compete, he'll teach you to recognize your successes, redefine what it means to be a winner, and develop a strong character that will truly give you a competitive edge in all of life's games.